GET IN THE GAME

STEVE PIXLER

CONTINUUM
MINISTRY RESOURCES

Published in the United States of America in 2019 by

CONTINUUM MINISTRY RESOURCES

206 Cedar Rock Court

Mansfield, TX 76063

Copyright © 2019 Steve Pixler

ISBN 978—0—9914552—1—8

TABLE OF CONTENTS

INTRODUCTION

QUE SERA, SERA

I n June 1956, Alfred Hitchcock released the widely-acclaimed movie, *The Man Who Knew Too Much*. It was the story of a family caught in a web of international espionage ending with the kidnap and rescue of their young son. In the climactic scene where the boy is rescued, Jo McKenna, played by Doris Day, sings a song that would become the most memorable feature of the film, winning an Academy Award for the Best Original Song.

The song was called *Que Sera, Sera (Whatever Will Be, Will Be)*, and it became Doris Day's signature song. It became, as many described it, an "anthem of cheerful fatalism." Just roll with the punches because whatever will happen in life is simply going to happen anyway. No sense in getting wound up about it.

The phrase, *que sera, sera,* oddly enough, is not of Spanish origin. In fact, it's bad grammar in Spanish. People who study these things, bless them, say that *que sera, sera* is of English origin and can be traced back to the 1500's. It is thought to have been an idiomatic corruption of an Italian phrase indicating "whatever will be, will be." It was used on the crests of English nobility in both Spanish and Italian forms, though the phrase is grammatically incorrect in whatever language it's used.

Now you know.

It's interesting to me that Doris Day sang this "anthem of cheerful fatalism" in the aftermath of The Second World War to a generation that just wanted life to settle down to a bearable norm. Don't fight the inevitable—just put your head down and let fate have her way. Life is so much easier that way.

Yet, *Que Sera, Sera,* just like the movie, was performed as cheerful fatalism against the backdrop of desperate times. The 1950's were deceptively peaceful and prosperous. In reality, the *Leave It To Beaver* decade was just the postwar calm before the storm, the terrific cultural and political storm of the 1960's. Indeed, the 1960's and 70's were the fruit of the 1950's, the bills coming due on a generation that didn't want to face its demons. The soothing *"whatever will be"* mantra of the establishment gave way to a radical, rebellious uprising. The children of exhausted warriors were no longer content to sing *Que Sera, Sera.* They were furiously determined to bend "whatever will be" into "whatever *should* be."

They were not in the mood for *Que Sera, Sera*. And, after you read this, you'll not be either.

And here's what I'd like to do in this short book. I want to set you on fire. I want to rouse you out of your slumber, out of your *ennui*, out of your slump-shouldered surrender to a remorseless fate. You are not helpless, you are not hopeless. You have a role to play in the outcome of your situation. I want you to rip the words *Que Sera, Sera* off your lips, spit out the "whatever" phrases that have conditioned you to settle for anything life throws your way.

You are powerful; you are anointed; you are created and called by God for an eternal destiny. *"Whatever will be, will be"* is a load of horse manure. Stop mucking through the poo. Get out of the malaise, the doldrums, the funk that paralyzes your faith. It's time to rise up and tell good ol' Doris, bless her sweet heart, to hush up once and for all. Jesus didn't come to earth, die on the cross and cast out the devil just for you to sigh and sing *Que Sera, Sera*.

No way.

CHAPTER ONE

TWO MYTHS

People tend to believe two myths about life. First, we often think that we are spectators in the game of life, observers sitting in the stands watching The Fates play out the inevitable. Our job is to celebrate when we win and cuss when we lose.

Christians believe that, too, sort of. They just think that the players on the field are God and the devil. Most Christians have been trained to think that accepting an inevitable outcome is true Christian humility. We must simply surrender to God's sovereign, ineffable will. "God knows best," we mutter as we trudge helplessly out of the stadium. "Maybe things will go better next time."

We have been trained to believe that God is sovereign and we are not. Period. This means for many that we are called just to give up and give God glory when things go wrong. We display humility by suffering with dignity.

We twist Paul's words on being "content" in every circumstance (Philippians 4:11) into being resigned to our fate. But that's theological balderdash. Paul fought hard to change outcomes; and when he spoke of being "content," he meant that he was at peace inside while working hard to change the world outside.

Paul did *not* teach that we are to simply accept circumstances as the will of God and do nothing to shift outcomes. Paul taught us to "fight the good fight of faith, and lay hold on eternal life" (1 Timothy 6:12). He urged us to "put on the whole armor of God, that you may be able to stand against the schemes of the devil" (Ephesians 6:11). He declared that we "wrestle against principalities and powers, against the rulers of darkness and spiritual wickedness in high places" (Ephesians 6:12).

Paul spoke about "laboring fervently in prayer" (Colossians 4:12) and "struggling mightily" (Colossians 1:29) for the purpose of God in the world. He even said—in one of the single most breathtaking statements in Scripture—that he was "filling up what is lacking in Christ's afflictions for the sake of his body, that is, the church" (Colossians 1:24). Paul most definitely believed that we have a role to play in fulfilling the will and work of God in the earth.

Faith does not simply acquiesce. And contending for a miracle is *not* unbelief. Settling for the status quo is not humility—it is falling short of the promise (Hebrews 4:1). Unless the Father tells us to stop asking like he once told Paul (2 Corinthians 12:9), *we must keep reaching!*

We are not spectators.

The second myth we believe is that God works instantly when—and if!—he works. We tend to believe that miracles are instantaneous. We have been conditioned to believe that divine intervention is— BAM!—a lightning bolt out of the sky, dramatic and instant. We pray for God to move in our situation, and when things don't happen instantly we assume God is not at work. Then, we either experience deep disappointment and become disillusioned with God, or we develop theologies to explain why God isn't working and why we should just accept the outcome as "the will of God."

Both of these myths are wrong. Dead wrong. First, you are not a spectator, not an observer. You are a player in the game. You have a role to play in the outcome. Whether you win or lose largely depends on your willingness to get in the game. You are called to be a partner with Christ, not just one who applauds him from the nosebleeds.

Second, God works through process. Most miracles —yes, *most!*—do not happen suddenly. Most miracles are miracles in slow motion, miracles that happen over time as God walks us through the problem into a solution. God allows (not *causes*) problems in our life because problems are the matrix of divine-human relationship. God reveals his faithfulness to us, his character and nature, person and power, through the problems we face.

And problems not only reveal God to us—problems reveal who we are to ourselves. For God, problems are never really a problem. They are simply opportunities to make his mighty power known and strengthen us in our faith toward him. For God, relationship matters most; and relationships take time.

Think about Jesus turning water to wine. This was one of those miracles that happened suddenly: the servants filled the pots with water, and the water became wine. *Voila*. But the truth is Jesus turns water to wine every single day. It happens every day, everywhere, all over the planet.

Think about it. That's what wine *is*—water turned to wine. Water that flows from the earth into the roots of the vine, out into the branches, into the cluster and into the grape. The grape is harvested, crushed, fermented and stored for years in barrels. Then, it's bottled, labeled, shipped, sold and poured into your glass.

It's a miracle! The water has become wine.

No different from the wedding at Cana—except for *time*. What made the miracle in Jesus' day notable was that the process was accelerated dramatically, and the water became wine in a moment. But, if you think about it, the miracle in slow motion is no less a miracle.

And when we see miracles in slow motion, we tend to see them as unanswered prayers. We often allow the spirit of disappointment to embitter our heart, and we stop reaching for the answer. That's too bad! We often give up just before the answer comes.

The truth is, God works through *people*, and God works through *process*. And that's the two aspects of God's work that I want to talk about for a bit.

CHAPTER TWO

GOD WORKS THROUGH PEOPLE

God works through people. He does so by his own design and decision. God doesn't work through people because he must; he works through people because that's what he chose to do. And when you're God, you get to do what you want. Pretty cool, huh?

Look at Psalm 115:3:

"Our God is in the heavens; he does all that he pleases."

This is one of the strongest statements of God's sovereignty in the Bible. "He does all that he pleases." And yet it pleased him to partner with people. It pleased him to create humans in his image and likeness and to share his sovereignty over the world with you and me.

Thirteen verses down, Psalm 115:16 goes on to say,

"The heavens are the Lord's heavens, but the earth he has given to the children of man."

God does what he pleases, and it pleased him to give mankind dominion over the earth.

Here's how the Creator put it:

Then God said, "Let us make man in our image, after our likeness. And let them have dominion over the fish of the sea and over the birds of the heavens and over the livestock and over all the earth and over every creeping thing that creeps on the earth." So God created man in his own image, in the image of God he created him; male and female he created them.

And God blessed them. And God said to them, "Be fruitful and multiply and fill the earth and subdue it, and have dominion over the fish of the sea and over the birds of the heavens and over every living thing that moves on the earth." (Genesis 1:26–28)

God gave humans dominion over the earth as an expression of his image. This is one of the ways in which people are *like* God: we are sovereign over the realm God assigned us. And God respects this sovereignty. He does not violate mankind's rule. He does not intervene in human affairs without a human request. *This is why we pray.*

Think about it: prayer is an absurdity if God already does whatever he wants in the human realm without an invitation. Why ask?

When God gets ready to move in the world, he looks for a Noah, who is "perfect in his generations" (Genesis 6:9). He searches through heaven and earth to find a person to "stand in the gap and make up the hedge" (Ezekiel 22:30). He looks through heaven for one "worthy to open the book" of his covenant promises (Revelation 5:2). God actively recruits people to partner with his purpose:

> *"For the eyes of the Lord run to and fro throughout the whole earth, to give strong support to those whose heart is blameless toward him" (2 Chronicles 16:9).*

God works through people!

One of the most astonishing word pictures in the Bible is where Jesus "stands at the door and knocks" (Revelation 3:20). What?! The Creator of heaven and earth does not need to knock on anybody's door. In fact, Jesus already proved he can just walk *through* the door, if he wants. *He does not need to knock!*

Yet he knocks. Why? Because God respects order. He refuses to violate dominion. The one Being in the universe who has the power to be the greatest control freak of all is the one Being who most insistently refuses to control anyone. It seems clear that love requires freedom; and since God *is* love, he will not violate freedom.

Remember the story of Peter being delivered from prison by an angel? (Acts 12) The angel opens every impregnable door in the story—even the iron gate that led to the city!—but not the weakest one: the puny little door at Mary's house. God will remove every obstacle to your deliverance except the last one: the door to your own heart. *You* must open that door.

The incarnation of God in Christ is the single greatest proof that God works through people. God's Son, our Lord Jesus Christ, became a human to save humans. God did not violate human dominion to reclaim his good creation; rather, he came to earth *as a human* to save the world. The first Adam surrendered his dominion to sin and death, and only the last Adam could restore human dominion to its original partnership with God.

Take time to read this lengthy quote and cogitate on the staggering implications:

Have this mind among yourselves, which is yours in Christ Jesus, who, though he was in the form of God, did not count equality with God a thing to be grasped, but emptied himself, by taking the form of a servant, being born in the likeness of men. And being found in human form, he humbled himself by becoming obedient to the point of death, even death on a cross.

Therefore God has highly exalted him and bestowed on him the name that is above every name, so that at the name of Jesus every knee should bow, in heaven and on earth and under the earth, and every tongue confess that Jesus Christ is Lord, to the glory of God the Father. (Philippians 2:5–11)

Note the descent-ascent-descent circular movement:

(1) Jesus descended to earth and was "found in human form." He "humbled himself."

(2) Then, God "highly exalted him" and restored divine-human dominion over the earth as Jesus ascended to the throne of God in heaven. The Son of God came down to earth as a man, as God in flesh, then ascended back to heaven *still as a man.* This means that Jesus redeemed human dominion over the earth and gained the additional glory of dominion over *heaven, earth and under-earth.* As Jesus put it, "All authority has been given to me in heaven and in earth" (Matthew 28:18)

(3) Then, at Pentecost, Jesus poured out the Holy Spirit into the hearts of believers, bringing heaven and earth into alignment through the church. Once again, God came to dwell on earth through people, gathering believers from all over the world into the

Spirit-filled, God-indwelled body of Christ. *God works through people!*

Read Mark 16:19–20 carefully:

So then the Lord Jesus, after he had spoken to them, was taken up into heaven and sat down at the right hand of God. And they went out and preached everywhere, while the Lord worked with them and confirmed the message by accompanying signs.

Look at the divine-human partnership in this passage: Jesus ascended into heaven and "sat down at the right hand of God." That is another way of saying that Jesus was seated on the throne of God with *all* the authority of God the Father at his disposal. Jesus, the eternal Son of God, the living expression of God's glory, the visible image of the Father, rules *as God* over all creation.

But that's only half the equation—Jesus also rules *as a human*. Jesus is the living interface between God and man, the bridge, the mediator between the divine and the human. As Paul said, "For there is one God, and there is one mediator between God and men, the man Christ Jesus" (1 Timothy 2:5). In Christ, all creation is reconciled to and united with its Creator.

Jesus rules as a human so humans can rule with him. He opened the door and made a way for humans to share in the divine life of God and govern all creation with God, which was the Creator's original intent. So, while celebrating the enthronement of Christ, don't overlook *your* role in the rest of the story. Jesus ascended into heaven to rule as both God and man. But he also poured out the Holy Spirit into believers so that *you* could work in partnership with the Father in Christ through the power of the Holy Spirit.

Jesus didn't come to earth just so God could experience being a man, and he didn't ascend into heaven just so he could rule as a man. He came to earth and ascended back to heaven *for you.* (In fact, he did so *as you.*) Jesus came so *you* could be one with God and rule with Christ over heaven, earth and under-earth.

Mark 16 again:

- "They went out and preached everywhere."

- "The Lord worked with them and confirmed the message by accompanying signs."

Look at the partnership. Look at the synergy, the cooperation, the unity, the alignment, the whatever-other-word-you-can-think-of to describe how *God works through people.*

When Jesus poured out the Holy Spirit, he brought the human race into union with the Father. As Paul put it, "God has sent the Spirit of his Son into our hearts, crying, "Abba! Father!" (Galatians 4:6) We are reconciled to God through Christ. Now, divine-human partnership is possible.

It is important to see the role of the Holy Spirit in this equation lest we think that our effort in cooperation with God is just our effort, mere human effort, fleshly works that attempt to earn divine status through righteous performance. No way, not at all. Without the Holy Spirit, we could never partner with the Father. We have no power or strength in the flesh to accomplish anything remotely divine.

But the Father fixed that problem when he sent the Spirit of Jesus into our heart, the Helper, the *Parakletos*, the one called alongside, the Comforter, the Holy Spirit. Now, because we are sanctified and empowered by the Holy Spirit, we are united with the Father in Christ. We are aligned in partnership with God. Through the incarnation, ascension and outpouring of Jesus through the Holy Spirit, *God can now work through people.*

When we hear the gospel, the Holy Spirit resurrects our dead human spirit. (Ephesians 2:1, 5) When we come alive, we believe the gospel. Faith is God's gift to us. The Holy Spirit opens up a well of God's Presence in our human spirit, and the faith of Jesus ignites our faith. Our human spirit, now alive through the life of God, flows up through our soul and out through our body. Our entire human being is transformed by the indwelling Spirit of God. The Holy Spirit empowers our human spirit and gives us the capacity to partner with God.

Catch the synergy here: our human spirit is now infused with God's Holy Spirit. Our emotions, will and mind are set free to voluntarily obey the will of God. We are free now to manifest our eternal destiny. The enslaved human will, once inextricably bound to the lies of Satan, who took us captive at his will (2 Timothy 2:26) and dehumanized us through sin (Romans 1:18-31), is now liberated to fulfill its original purpose as the image of God in the world.

When God sets us free, we freely choose to do his will, for our will was created to express the will of God. *That's what re-humanized humans do—they believe and obey!* And since God is love, his will is not forced on us. He frees us to love him in return, which we do naturally when we encounter his love. "We love him because he first loved us" (1 John 4:19).

The resurrected human spirit was the missing element throughout the Old Testament era. The people of Israel under the Law of Moses could not do the will of God because their human spirit was enslaved to sin and death.

But Jesus broke the power of sin and death at the cross and came to dwell in our heart through the Holy Spirit. His resurrected and glorified human spirit, fully indwelled by the Spirit of the Father, erupted like a geyser within our human spirit, becoming a "spring of water welling up to eternal life" (John 4:14). As Jesus said, "Whoever believes in me, as the Scripture has said, 'Out of his heart will flow rivers of living water'" (John 7:38). Jesus infused the Spirit of the Living God into our hearts.

Our partnership with God is possible because our human spirit is infused and empowered with the Holy Spirit. Jesus prayed in John 17 that we would be one with the Father just as he is one with the Father.

> *"I do not ask for these only, but also for those who will believe in me through their word, that they may all be one, just as you, Father, are in me, and I in you, that they also may be in us, so that the world may believe that you have sent me. The glory that you have given me I have given to them, that they may be one even as we are one, I in them and you in me, that they may become perfectly one, so that the world may know that you sent me and loved them even as you loved me.* (John 17:20–23)

Look closely at the key phrases:

- "That they may all be one, just as you, Father, are in me, and I in you."

- "That they also may be in us, so that the world may believe that you have sent me."

- "That they may be one even as we are one, I in them and you in me, that they may become perfectly one."

Our oneness with God (and with one another) is possible because we are baptized into Christ and share his union with the Father through the Holy Spirit. This oneness, called *perichoresis* by theologians (they say the darnedest things!), is the interfusion of being that the godhead shares. Perichoresis literally means "interpenetration." The Father, Son and Holy Spirit are distinct within the eternal life of God, but they are one divine being, sharing the existential interpenetration of divine life.

Whew. That was a mouthful.

Jesus prayed that believers would be one with God "even as we (Jesus and the Father) are one." The same internal, eternal perichoretic union that unites the godhead draws us into the eternal life of the godhead: the Father indwelling Jesus and Jesus indwelling us ("I in them and you in me").

The goal of creation has always been that "God may be all in all" (1 Corinthians 15:28). The people of God are "the fullness of him (God) who fills all in all" (Ephesians 1:23). Perfect union with God and his people—and through his people, perfect union with all creation—has been God's goal all along.

God plans to fill all people in the new creation with his indwelling Presence, and through his people to mediate his indwelling Presence into every corner of the resurrected universe. And through the resurrection of Jesus in the middle of history and through the outpouring of the Holy Spirit at Pentecost, the work of new creation has already begun. The future is now.

Paul describes the purpose of everything as,

"His purpose, which he set forth in Christ as a plan for the fullness of time, to unite all things in him, things in heaven and things on earth." (Ephesians 1:10)

Christ Jesus is the bridge, the interface, that unites all creation with the Father. The Holy Spirit, who is the Spirit of Jesus and the Father within us, brings us into perfect union with the godhead. And—though this is a topic for another time—this is how believers are made one with each other.

Oneness with God and with each other is how the Presence of God floods the nations until, as the prophet declared, "the earth [is] filled with the knowledge of the glory of the Lord as the waters cover the sea" (Habakkuk 2:14). This is how the prayer is answered, "Your kingdom come, your will be done on earth as it is in heaven" (Matthew 6:10).

The Holy Spirit was given to allow us to partner with God without attempting any longer to produce the will of God out of a fallen, sinful heart. God made a New Covenant with us that wrote his law upon our regenerated hearts, giving us the power to fulfill the law through love by the Spirit.

As you're gathering by now, the New Testament is chock-full of references describing how God works through people.

Want more? Here's a zinger:

"We are God's fellow workers." (1 Corinthians 3:9)

This incredible statement reveals the importance of divine-human *synergy*. God works with us, and we work with God. (Theologians call this the interplay of *monergism* and *synergism*, but we will let them expound that on their own time.) The important thing for us to grasp is that God works through people. We are not spectators. We are not mere observers, victims caught in the remorseless grip of fate. We have a role to play in our circumstances.

We can call in the miraculous power of God. We have the power of prayer, praise and prophecy to break the stymied, frustrated flow of human history. We don't have to just stand by and watch all hell break loose in our world. We can stand upright, square our shoulders and use the authority we have been given to pray heaven into earth.

It's time to get in the game!

Yet we do not play the game alone. When I was a kid, I would hear the preachers cry out, voices trembling, fists punctuating the air, hot tears flowing, "Work out your own salvation with *fear and trembling!*" And I tried. I tried my best to work my salvation out. And I did it fervently with an extra dose of fear and trembling. I was darn near scared to death. But working it out never worked.

Then, one day, I don't remember what made me go there, I actually the read the entire quote in context. What I saw shocked me. Then it made me mad. I had been scared into a frenzy since childhood with a half quote, with a scripture pulled out of context and twisted to say *exactly the opposite* of what it says. Here's Paul's whole statement:

> *Work out your own salvation with fear and trembling, for it is God who works in you, both to will and to work for his good pleasure. (Philippians 2:12–13)*

Work out your own salvation...*for it is God who works in you!* That changes everything. This scripture shows an incredible balance of divine-human synergy, a cooperation between God and us that *works*. We work out our own salvation as God works in us.

Two things: (1) We are not required to work alone; (2) God will not work without us. We *work* as he *works* in us. We are not sent out on the field to play the game alone. But neither do we sit in the stands while God plays the game for us. We play the game in partnership with God. We play the game through the empowering Presence of God in us through the Holy Spirit.

Paul says this kind of thing all through his writings. Here's another example:

Now to him who is able to do far more abundantly than all that we ask or think, according to the power at work within us. (Ephesians 3:20)

God is able to do more than we can imagine, but he will do *everything* he does through the "power at work within us," which is the power of God himself through the Holy Spirit in us. God never asks us to do the work without him, but neither will he do the work without us.

Yet another example:

For this I toil, struggling with all his energy that he powerfully works within me. (Colossians 1:29)

You've got to look close at this—don't skim the scripture just because you've read it before. Mediate on this:

(1) "For this I toil, struggling..."

(2) "...with all his energy that *he* powerfully works within *me*."

Look at the blend, the synergy, of *he* and *me*.

You can't do the work without God, but he will not do it without *you*. You move the ball down the field when you believe the promises of God and take action to live them out. Paul said that the promises of God find their fulfillment through God's "yes" and our "amen":

For all the promises of God find their Yes in him. That is why it is through him that we utter our Amen to God for his glory. (2 Corinthians 1:20)

God proclaims a "Yes!" promise over our life, and we respond *through Christ* with an emphatic, "Amen!" Our response seals the deal. And our response is a perichoretic response blending the faith of Jesus with our now regenerated faith. We say "amen" *through* Christ.

We cannot simply sit idly by and hope for the best. We must intentionally partner with the promises of God. We must receive and rehearse the promise and declare it daily. The word of faith must be "in our mouth" (Romans 10:8). We put his "Yes!" word in our mouth and shout, "Amen!" when we pray, praise and prophesy the promises of God.

We play the game through:

(1) Prayer

(2) Praise

(3) Prophecy

You are not a victim. You are not a helpless pawn of fate. You have a role to play in the outcome of the game. You walk by *faith*, not by *fate*. It's time to rehearse the promises you have been given and start declaring and decreeing what God said will do. Say "amen!" to his "yes!"

Speak over your children, over your marriage, over your finances. Stop speaking anything that is less than an "amen" to God's promise. Stop channeling fear and doubt. Renounce worry, which is just faith in a lie. Get a grip. Get mad. Get determined. *Get in the game!*

CHAPTER THREE

GOD WORKS THROUGH PROCESS

HUMAN FREEDOM

Most people tend to believe that God acts unilaterally in the world, that miracles are an abrupt divine intervention over which humans have no control. When God does not intervene abruptly and fix all the world's problems in a moment, this misunderstanding of an instant-all-at-once-work-of-God can bring either bitter frustration with God's inaction or a jaded cynicism that resigns us all to our fate. The dominant attitude becomes "*whatever.*"

Much of the anger toward God in the world today comes from the philosophical idea that a good God would not allow evil. If he's God, then he is by definition "all-powerful." And since he is all-powerful, then why does he allow evil continue? How can a good God stand by and watch a little girl get raped and murdered and do nothing about it? Or, even worse, why does he intervene to prevent some atrocities and not others?

This question has been asked countless times since Christians first started preaching that God is good. Ancient pagans never had a problem with this question because they already believed that the gods were both good and evil, strong but not all-powerful. But Christians preached that the one true God is both *great* and *good*. And that creates "the problem of evil."

Now, I don't for a moment think that I can settle millennia of arguments in one short book. But I can tell you that I wrestled with this question as a young man to the point of doubting the existence of God. I struggled with believing that God could be good and allow evil to exist. It was a real issue for me for a few years.

And then, as I grew older, I experienced pain that made "the problem of evil" much less philosophical and much more personal. The death of our first child, deep financial losses, ministry failure and intense personal attacks brought my anger toward God boiling to the surface. I honestly felt at times like I hated him. He had all the power, and I had none. I loathed that powerless feeling.

I'll tell you the story someday.

But all I know is that repeated encounters with the Father transformed my heart. I read countless books on "the problem of evil," but what finally delivered my mind from the paralyzing grip of uncertainty was not theology or philosophy. It was personal encounters with the Presence of God. I came away believing that God is both good and great.

And, though I have to admit that I don't have answers that will fully satisfy every question, I came away from those encounters with the growing conviction that God created the world out of love and love requires freedom.

This means God works in the world *as it is*, not as we wish it was.

If God intervenes in every free human action—if he prevents us from experiencing the real consequences of our freedom—then the world becomes a quite different place than he intended. It becomes the habitat of humans on a string, puppet people who simply do whatever God moves them to do. That's not freedom, and that's not love.

God created humans free and gave us dominion over the world. We freely chose to surrender our dominion to sin and death, to the power of evil. That's where the problem of evil comes from—from the Evil One. Adam chose to partner with the Evil One. We're in this mess because we chose it. We have to stop blaming God for what we allowed and the devil caused.

Yet God refused to abandon us to our fate. And he did not strip us of our dominion. He remained committed to the idea that people should manifest his image and share in his rule over creation. Rather than bail on his original plan, God freely chose to send his Son to earth as a fully free human to break the power of evil over humans and restore our dominion to its original partnership with God.

God's plan for us is that we should bear his image and share his glory by ruling over all creation with him. If he simply does the work for us, then we are still detached observers who just applaud when God does mighty things. But God doesn't need our applause. He didn't create the universe just so we would give him a standing ovation. He desires glory, no doubt, but he doesn't want it alone—the Creator wants us to share in his glory. God will not *give* his glory to another, but he will *share* it.

> *"What is man that you are mindful of him, and the son of man that you care for him? Yet you have made him a little lower than the heavenly beings and crowned him with glory and honor. You have given him dominion over the works of your hands; you have put all things under his feet."* *(Psalm 8:4–6)*

God created us, crowned us with *"glory and honor,"* and gave us *"dominion"* over the works of his hands. Paul said that the Spirit of God within us is "Christ in you, the hope of glory" (Colossians 1:27). To be saved and raised in the resurrection at the last day is to be "glorified" (Romans 8:3). The writer of Hebrews says that salvation is "bringing many sons to glory" (Hebrews 2:10).

God wants us to share in his glory.

One aspect of glory is responsibility. God created us to share in his rule over creation. He made us *responsible.* We were responsible for the mess, so we are responsible for the clean up. Yet, since we did not have the power to clean up the mess we made, Jesus came to clean the mess up for us and *as us.* And by filling us with his Holy Spirit, he came to clean up the mess *with us.*

If my son has homework, I may help with him with it. But I will not do it for him. Why? I love my son, and I want him to learn the math. I want him to be "glorified" by passing the math test and gaining competence for greater responsibility in the world.

My son doesn't really like that, but there you go.

God is fiercely determined to restore his fallen world and deliver his beloved people, but he will not do it without us. He intervenes in the world through us. He answers when we call. Every action of God in the world is a response to someone's prayer.

And even when we pray and God does intervene, he still works in the world *as it is*, not as we wish it was. He works through people—through their cooperation or their resistance—and he works against the powers of evil that still resist the victory of Christ.

Jesus defeated the powers of evil at the cross. He also purchased salvation for all people, everywhere, at all times. Yet evil powers still resist their inevitable dethronement, and humans still reject free salvation. In other words, the work of Jesus must still be worked out in the world.

This is why he ascended into heaven and poured out the Holy Spirit. In one sense, when Jesus cried, "It is finished!" on the cross, the work of salvation was fully complete. But in another sense, the work had just begun—the work of filling people with the Spirit of God so that, through people, God's good creation would be restored and all things made new.

Salvation is *altogether* the work of a sovereign God. Yet that sovereign God chose to work through us. Even as he works through us, it is *him* working in us. In other words, even the work we do in partnership with him is still his sovereign grace at work in us. We cannot save ourselves through our own power. So, God fills us with *his* power and completes his sovereign work of salvation through us.

And this sovereign work of salvation in us and through us is done in the real world. God influences people, but he does not control them. Just as often as the Bible states that salvation is the work of grace alone, it states that we must respond to that grace. While we cannot produce righteousness out of our own human strength, we can produce unrighteousness. We can resist the grace of God and refuse to obey. The countless warnings in scripture against disobedience show that disobedience is a real possibility.

This means that our prayers must take into account the free decision of humans. We must craft prayers that are strategic and targeted toward influencing human hearts. We have to know how to discern the spiritual powers dominating human hearts, cast them out and deliver humans to encounter the love of God. If they can encounter God's love, their heart can be turned. That's just how powerful the love of God is.

But prayer is not manipulation. Prayer is not coercion. Prayer is not witchcraft. Prayer is not us trying to control people with the mighty power of God. Prayer must be the release of love, the free encounter of God's goodness. That is the only thing that truly changes people.

Humans were given dominion over creation, but not over other people. Dominion over people is domination, and that's demonic. Jesus told his disciples,

> *The kings of the Gentiles exercise lordship over them, and those in authority over them are called benefactors. But not so with you. Rather, let the greatest among you become as the youngest, and the leader as one who serves. (Luke 22:25–26)*

You have dominion, but not domination. This means that you have authority to stand as a son or daughter of God and release God's love into every situation. You can call on the Spirit of the Most High God to influence the hearts of people through love. You have the authority to affect outcomes. That's what strategic, targeted prayer does.

So then, think about how much we stand by and watch people make bad decisions without knowing how to help them through targeted prayer. We just stand by, cursing helplessly, while they plunge into foolish, even deadly, decisions.

We must get in the game!

We must learn how to pray prayers that take human freedom into account. We must learn how to pray prayers that invite the Father into the lives of the people we love—not to control them, but to liberate them through love.

God works in the world, but he works in the world *as it is*. And it is a world defined by human freedom. That's how God made it. And effective prayers take both the inviolability of human freedom and the power of God's transforming love into account. Discerning prayer warriors know that people must freely choose to obey, but they also know that God's love breaks down every barrier and liberates the human heart.

So we must keep praying. Get in the game! When answers don't come, and people refuse to play fair; when situations get complicated and adversaries harden their heart; when humans choose resistance over surrender, righteous people just keep on praying. We do not give up. We do not stumble weakly off the field. The discerning prayer warrior stays in the game, to wildly jumble up my metaphors.

Don't blame God when people refuse to do his will. Ask God to press in closer. Ask him to schedule a divine encounter that will rock their world. Just keep on asking for the love of God to wrap them up and change their heart. Stay in the game!

Use the authority you have been given as a son or daughter of God. You have dominion—exercise it. Wield it. Play the game. Speak to the mountain. Tell the mountain what to do. Speak to the hardness of heart. Summon the release of divine love. Ask for a divine encounter. And don't stop asking, decreeing and

declaring until reality bends, shifts and shapes in
response to the love of God mediated through *your*
intercession.

CHAPTER FOUR

SPIRITUAL WARFARE

B ut there's another layer to the process, more than just mere human freedom. The world is dominated by dark forces that enslave the human will, and God works within that dark reality, the light shining in darkness.

Human resistance to the will of God is often hardened by demonic control. And, no matter how much we would love for him to do so, God does not simply snap his fingers and—poof!—all demonic powers evaporate. That would be nice, but it's simply not how God works. Again, he works in the world as it is, not as we wish it was.

As Paul put it when writing about cantankerous people,

> *God may perhaps grant them repentance leading to a knowledge of the truth, and they may come to their senses and escape from the snare of the devil, after being captured by him to do his will. (2 Timothy 2:25–26)*

People are "captured by [the devil] to do his will." God enters the fray and fights for their soul. He does so by granting them repentance that leads to a knowledge of the truth; the truth breaks the power of the lie, they come to their senses and escape Satan's snare. There's a great deal of uncertainty in all that, and a boatload of real suspense. It is a real battle for human souls, not just the pretense of it.

The devil uses "the power of death" and "the fear of death" to manipulate and enslave humans:

> *Since therefore the children share in flesh and blood, he himself likewise partook of the same things, that through death he might destroy the one who has the power of death, that is, the devil, and deliver all those who through fear of death were subject to lifelong slavery. (Hebrews 2:14–15)*

The devil enslaves humans. Jesus came to destroy the devil and set humans free.

John the apostle said,

> *Whoever makes a practice of sinning is of the devil, for the devil has been sinning from the beginning. The reason the Son of God appeared was to destroy the works of the devil. 1 John 3:8 (ESV):*

People under the power of sin are aligned with the devil. They probably don't know it, and most likely don't intend it, but they are playing for the wrong team. And their will is captive to the power of sin. Only the love of God can liberate their will. And Jesus came to do just that: "destroy the works of the devil" by delivering people from his control.

So, when we pray for people and summon a divine encounter, we are setting up a clash between the love of God and lust of sin. And, while the love of God is overwhelming, God's sovereign decision to preserve human freedom means that the person loved by God must respond freely to his love.

God will not overwhelm people beyond their willingness to surrender. In the encounter, the Spirit of God creates a moment of awareness when the loved one must choose to follow. As Paul says in Romans, we must *yield* ("present ourselves") to the influence of the Holy Spirit. (Romans 6:13)

The Spirit of God creates a divine encounter. The heart of the person must freely choose. Yet, to thicken the plot, there are always dark forces at work to hinder the right choice. Paul said to the Thessalonians,

> *We wanted to come to you—I, Paul, again and again—but Satan hindered us. (1 Thessalonians 2:18)*

Paul preached and worked in an arena of real resistance to the kingdom of God. He knew that the powers of evil were real. But he pushed back. He did not walk dejectedly off the field and forfeit the game. Paul fought the good fight of faith!

The discerning prayer warrior realizes that demonic forces must be authoritatively bound and restrained from working. We must "bind the strongman" before we can "plunder the strongman's house" (Mark 3:27). And the discerning prayer warrior knows that restraining the enemy is often a protracted, real-world battle. This is why he or she refuses to stop praying.

Jesus gave the church authority over all the power of the enemy because he knew we would need it.

> And he said to them, "I saw Satan fall like lightning from heaven. Behold, I have given you authority to tread on serpents and scorpions, and over all the power of the enemy, and nothing shall hurt you. Nevertheless, do not rejoice in this, that the spirits are subject to you, but rejoice that your names are written in heaven." (Luke 10:18–20)

The sense of Jesus' words in the original language is, "While you were preaching, I saw Satan falling like lightning from heaven." The preaching of the disciples had influence on the balance of power in the world *as it was*. The powers of darkness were defeated as the disciples played the game.

When we pray for people, preach to people and work to lead people to follow Christ, we must be aware of the spiritual reality in which God is working. He works in the world *as it is*, not as we wish it was. God works in a world filled with demonic resistance to his will.

Spiritual warfare is a real thing. I know that spiritual warfare can be exaggerated, even idolized, but the opposite error of blind denial is not helpful. There is a real war going on for the future, and we must understand what we are up against.

The classic passage on spiritual warfare is Ephesians 6:

> *Finally, be strong in the Lord and in the strength of his might. Put on the whole armor of God, that you may be able to stand against the schemes of the devil.*
>
> *For we do not wrestle against flesh and blood, but against the rulers, against the authorities, against the cosmic powers over this present darkness, against the spiritual forces of evil in the heavenly places.*
>
> *Therefore take up the whole armor of God, that you may be able to withstand in the evil day, and having done all, to stand firm.*
>
> *Stand therefore, having fastened on the belt of truth, and having put on the breastplate of righteousness, and, as shoes for your feet, having put on the readiness given by the gospel of peace. In all circumstances take up the shield of faith, with which you can extinguish all the flaming*

darts of the evil one; and take the helmet of salvation, and the sword of the Spirit, which is the word of God, praying at all times in the Spirit, with all prayer and supplication.

To that end, keep alert with all perseverance, making supplication for all the saints, and also for me, that words may be given to me in opening my mouth boldly to proclaim the mystery of the gospel, for which I am an ambassador in chains, that I may declare it boldly, as I ought to speak. (Ephesians 6:10–20)

Look at our opponents in the arena:

(1) We must stand against the schemes of the devil

(2) We do not wrestle with "flesh and blood" (humans)

(3) We wrestle against the "rulers, authorities and cosmic powers over this present darkness and the spiritual forces of evil in the heavenly places."

We are not in a fight with people. That's important to know. Our battle is with the devil and "the Powers." ("The Powers" is theological shorthand for all the antagonists listed in #3. The Powers are often called "the principalities and powers" from the King James Version rendering.) Paul's mention of "the devil" and "the Powers" indicates that we are in a struggle against the demonic realm and an array of fallen angels that were given rule over the nations after Noah's Flood.

Moses described when the Powers took control:

When the Most High gave to the nations their inheritance, when he divided mankind, he fixed the borders of the peoples according to the number of the sons of God. But the Lord's portion is his people, Jacob his allotted heritage. (Deuteronomy 32:8–9)

God divided mankind at Babel after the Flood, and he gave the nations over to "the sons of God," who were angels created to serve mankind but rebelled against that assignment and became "the gods" of the ancient world. The Lord God gave the nations over to idols due to their rebellion at Babel; but he kept Israel, the children of Abraham, for himself as his own inheritance. Sadly, Israel rejected the one true God, turned to idols and came under the domination of the Powers in the Exile.

When Jesus came to earth, one of the his primary assignments was to disempower and dethrone the Powers. He stripped them of their authority at the cross, and then ascended into heaven where he now rules over them all.

Yet the Powers refuse to willingly obey. They stubbornly resist the rule of Christ and continue to dominate human society. The Powers are still at work in the world through human systems and structures. The Powers work through human political, religious and cultural structures.

Wherever humans gather, at every intersection of human relations, the Powers hover waiting for an opportunity to exploit human list, greed and pride so that human dominion may be usurped. The Powers are parasitic, demonic forces that influence and enslave humans through deluded self-interest. The "Faustian bargain" is not a myth.

Paul calls the human systems and structures that the Powers exploit the "*stoicheia*."

> *See to it that no one takes you captive by philosophy and empty deceit, according to human tradition, according to the elemental spirits (stoicheia) of the world, and not according to Christ. (Colossians 2:8)*

Stoicheia is a Greek word that's tough to capture in English, which is why is it rendered so many different ways in various translations. But the basic idea is that *stoicheia* are the "spirit-systems" that govern human institutions and organizations.

As we know, every human organization has a "spirit." When two or more humans assemble, they blend into a collective human consciousness, forming a whole greater than the sum of its parts. This is where we get "mob mentality." People will do in a group what they would never do alone.

Neuroscientists tells us that human brains connect through a sort of mental WiFi, a process called "mirroring" where people influence each other mentally without knowing it. When "two or three get together," they create mental synergy.

And this synergy creates a spiritual space where invisible spirits can join the group. Jesus promised to gather with believers just like this:

For where two or three are gathered in my name, there am I among them." (Matthew 18:20)

The KJV says that Jesus will be "in the midst." Literally, when we form a group of two or three, we create a spiritual "middle" where Jesus can stand with us in actual, personal Presence.

And, in one truly astonishing statement, Paul even indicated that other humans can join the group remotely:

For though absent in body, I am present in spirit; and as if present, I have already pronounced judgment on the one who did such a thing. When you are assembled in the name of the Lord Jesus and my spirit is present, with the power of our Lord Jesus. (1 Corinthians 5:3–4)

Elisha told his servant the same thing: "Did not my heart go with you?" (2 Kings 5:26) This quite literally means that Elisha was present with Gehazi, his servant, as he pursued Naaman. Crazy, huh?!

People, that is truly beyond my understanding, right there. Maybe we can talk about it more another time.

Regardless, when humans gather, spiritual space is created in the "middle." This is, legally, neurologically and spiritually, the act of "incorporation," when two or more people become one entity, one "corpus," one body.

Frighteningly, this spiritual reality is also true in an evil sense. When humans gather, evil spirits are drawn to the "middle." The Powers look for opportunities to step into the intersections of human interaction to influence human behavior. As they gain dominance over humans by provoking and exploiting lust, the Powers take dominion over human institutions.

The Powers gain control over the *stoicheia,* over religion, politics, the economy, education, corporations, governments, media, the judicial system, neighborhoods, churches, families and organizations. The Powers grow in authority through surrendered human institutions until they dominate entire regions. People become like puppets on a string, manipulated and controlled by institutional spirits they cannot see and probably don't even believe in. This is how the Evil One gains control over the world.

But it is also how the power of the Evil One is broken. The "middle" is redeemed when Jesus steps in. When humans hear the gospel and believe, their allegiance is shifted to Christ. Every realm of influence under their control comes under the Lordship of Jesus. And this happens through love, not power. The Powers are cast out through love as humans reclaim their dominion in partnership with Christ. Humans repudiate their allegiance to the Powers, which masquerade as idols, and bow their knee to Jesus, the one true Lord.

That's powerful!

Do not miss this significance of this fact: Jesus came to disempower and dethrone the Powers. At the cross, the Powers wielded their greatest weapon against him: death. And, through his resurrection, Jesus broke the power of the Powers. And, since he was human, he also stripped the Powers of the stolen authority they usurped from Adam. Jesus recovered our dominion!

Paul said,

[God] disarmed the rulers and authorities and put them to open shame, by triumphing over them in him. (Colossians 2:15)

Paul again,

[God] raised him from the dead and seated him at his right hand in the heavenly places, far above all rule and authority and power and dominion, and above every name that is named, not only in this age but also in the one to come. (Ephesians 1:20–21)

Peter said,

[Jesus] has gone into heaven and is at the right hand of God, with angels, authorities, and powers having been subjected to him. (1 Peter 3:22)

Jesus said,

Fear not, I am the first and the last, and the living one. I died, and behold I am alive forevermore, and I have the keys of Death and Hades. (Revelation 1:17–18)

Jesus holds the keys we lost. He came to triumph over the powers of darkness and liberate our fallen world.

One more powerful word from Jesus about his victory over the Powers:

"On this rock I will build my church, and the gates of hell shall not prevail against it. I will give you the keys of the kingdom of heaven, and whatever you bind on earth shall be bound in heaven, and

whatever you loose on earth shall be loosed in heaven." (Matthew 16:18–19)

Jesus made this statement while standing outside Caesarea Philippi near the Grotto of Pan, called "the gates of hell" by locals. He was also standing in the shadow of Mt. Hermon, where Jewish legend told of a conspiracy forged between fallen angels—the Powers! —to resist the rule of the Most High and corrupt the children of men.

(Read Michael Heiser, *Unseen Realm,* to learn more about the the Powers and Christ's victory over them all. Amazing book!)

Jesus took the keys and then gave them to us. The victory of Jesus over the Powers is a victory in which we must participate. The gates of hell cannot prevail against *the church*. That's you and me. Whatever *we* bind on earth shall be bound in heaven. We have a role to play in Christ's victory.

We need to get in the game.

CHAPTER FIVE

THE VICTORY IS NOW

C hrist's rule over the Powers must be actualized through us. Again, as we preach the gospel of the kingdom and baptize believers into the lordship of Jesus, the balance of power in the world shifts. The Powers who resist the inevitable victory of Christ are cast down from their tyrannical control of human culture and society, and the reign of Jesus gains loving, free influence over the nations.

There is a real contest. Yes, Jesus defeated the evil powers at the cross and stripped them of their authority over the nations; yet the evil powers still resist the inevitable victory of Christ. Look at what Jesus said,

All authority in heaven and on earth has been given to me. Go therefore and make disciples of all nations, baptizing them in the name of the Father and of the Son and of the Holy Spirit, teaching them to observe all that I have commanded you. And behold, I am with you always, to the end of the age." (Matthew 28:18–20)

Jesus was given "all authority" by the Father when he ascended into heaven. He rules as Lord of all creation right now. But then, Jesus charged his disciples to go and *actualize* his authority in the earth by discipling the hearts and lives of real people in the real world. Since humans were given dominion over the earth, humans must be the ones to enact restored dominion once again.

Jesus commissioned and authorized the church to baptize humans into the family of God as they renounce their allegiance to sin. When believers are baptized, they are "delivered...from the domain of darkness and transferred...to the kingdom of his beloved Son" (Colossians 1:13). This transfer of allegiance releases the authority of Christ over all into the nations. The people of the world are brought into faith in Christ, and the world changes with them. The kingdom of God advances and grows in the world as people are shifted from darkness to light.

When people change, cultures change. When cultures change, cities change, nations change, the world changes. This is how God works out the victory of Jesus in the real world.

Remember Jack Bauer on *24*? "The following events occur in real time." And, "I just need more time!" Jack was never content to be a bystander. Jack got in the game.

Jesus is Jack. And Jack lives in us. But the events must happen in real time. There is a victory already won that must yet be won in the world. And that takes time.

Time is part of the *process*.

Jesus received all authority in heaven and earth, yet there is still work to be done to actualize that authority. Jesus said, "I am with you always, to the end of the age." Jesus is in us working through us to expand the borders of his kingdom in the world. Because Jesus has all authority, we are commissioned to disciple the nations, which are still under the oppressive tyranny of the Powers. When we arrive preaching that Jesus is Lord, baptizing and discipling those who believe, the Powers are emphatically overthrown.

Get the balance of this truth: Jesus won the victory, yet his victory is *still being won* in the real world right now.

Jesus is seated at the right hand of God the Father "until his enemies are made his footstool" (Psalm 110; 1 Corinthians 15:25; Hebrews 10:12, 13). This is why God sent forth the Spirit of Christ, the Victorious One, into our hearts—the finished victory must be finished through us.

As noted above, the Father "disarmed the rulers and authorities and put them to open shame, by triumphing over them in [Jesus]" (Colossians 2:15). Yet, the victory that Jesus won at the cross *for us* and *and us* is a victory that must be worked out *through us* in history.

All of the enemies of Jesus were subdued under his feet *legally,* but they must be subdued *actually.* The evil powers were legally evicted from the earth at the cross. The cry of Jesus, "It is finished!" was an official court order. But now Spirit-empowered believers are sent out as officers of the court to enforce the Notice to Vacate.

The "subduing" of Jesus' enemies—which are the Powers—prior to the Second Coming is one of the most emphasized ideas in the New Testament Scriptures. It is a theme that resonates through every chapter and verse, everywhere the kingdom of God is discussed. But 1 Corinthians 15 is the passage where Paul explains it with the most detail.

> *Then comes the end, when he delivers the kingdom to God the Father after destroying every rule and every authority and power. For he must reign until he has put all his enemies under his feet. The last enemy to be destroyed is death. (1 Corinthians 15:24–26)*

There are three things to draw out:

(1) Jesus will destroy the Powers.

(2) Jesus will reign until the Powers are subdued.

(3) The last enemy to be subdued is death itself, which happens at the Second Coming when Christ Jesus resurrects the dead.

This establishes the timeline of Christ's victory: he won total authority over the Powers at the cross; he ascended into heaven to be crowned King of kings and Lord of lords (Daniel 7:13, 14); then, he poured out the Holy Spirit so he can extend the reality of his rule from heaven to earth through us. "The end" will come when this work is done.

Jesus will reign from the right hand of God in heaven until all the Powers are destroyed and subdued under his feet. Then, after the Powers are subdued, death will be finally and fully defeated. Of course, Jesus defeated death at the cross just as he defeated the Powers. But Christ's victory over death must be actualized *in us* through the resurrection of all things when Jesus comes again.

The fact that death is clearly identified as "the last enemy" to be subdued establishes an indisputable timeline: the Powers will be subdued prior to the Second Coming. The victory of Christ's kingdom throughout the nations is underway *now*.

The church of Jesus proclaims the victory of Christ in every nation now, and those who believe are brought into allegiance to Christ's kingdom. As people shift their loyalty to Jesus, culture shifts slowly but surely, one person at a a time. And not out of violence or force, but out of love. And as culture shifts, the nations are transformed.

This takes time. And that's why we can't walk off the field. We must get in the game and stay in the game.

Jesus will present the victorious kingdom to the Father after he subdues and destroys the Powers. Remember, he came to "destroy the works of the devil." This is why he ascended to heaven, that he might rule from heaven and subdue his enemies under his feet through us. By ascending to the throne of God, Jesus received all authority in heaven and earth, the authority that we needed to reclaim our rightful dominion over the earth.

Jesus ruling "at the right hand of God" and "subduing his enemies under his feet" is an idea quoted from Psalm 110:

The Lord says to my Lord: "Sit at my right hand, until I make your enemies your footstool." (Psalm 110:1)

Psalm 110 was originally written about King David. But, in light of the resurrection of Jesus, the New Testament writers read Psalm 110 as the Father speaking to Christ promising to subdue every enemy under his feet. They saw the ascension of Jesus as his coronation at the right hand of God.

Here's an interesting fact: Psalm 110 is the Old Testament passage most-quoted in the New Testament. Psalm 110 shaped everything the earthly church thought about the mission of Jesus and the church in the world.

The early church believed that Jesus ascended into heaven to give humans on earth access to God's universal authority and power. (Ephesians 1:20-23; 2:6; Hebrews 10:19-22) They believed that Jesus remaining in heaven until the work is finished was actually essential to his mission. "The Lord says to my Lord: Sit at my right hand, until..." *Stay here until the work is done.*

Jesus seated at the right hand of the Father was a necessary part of winning global victory over the Powers. When Jesus ascended into heaven, he "omnipresenced" his victorious human spirit in the hearts of believers everywhere. This made the resurrected Jesus present wherever believers are present. So, when believers enter a home, a city, a nation, Jesus enters.

The Powers *hate* that.

Jesus told his disciples that it was actually better for them—"it is to your advantage"—for him to go away to heaven (John 16:7–11). The Holy Spirit, the Presence of the resurrected, glorified divine-human Jesus, could not come to dwell within the church as long as Jesus remained on the earth. Jesus was the personal tabernacle, the dwelling place, of God. But when he ascended, the church became "the dwelling place for God through the Spirit" (Ephesians 2:22).

Moreover, Jesus promised that believers would do "greater works" than he did because—get that *because!* —he ascended to the Father (John 14:12). The works are greater because the Presence of Jesus is multiplied and intensified as he fills believers all over the earth from heaven at "the right hand of the Father."

The early church preached that "heaven must receive [Jesus]" until the promised restoration of Israel foretold by the prophets. (Acts 3:21) Moreover, they believed that the promised restoration of Israel foretold by the prophets was already underway. Peter said,

And all the prophets who have spoken, from Samuel and those who came after him, also proclaimed these days. (Acts 3:24)

"These days" are the days foretold by the prophets when the enemies of Israel would be subdued. And as it turns out, the only way the human enemies of Israel could be subdued was for the spiritual enemies, the Powers behind human power, to be subdued. Rome,

the empire *de jure*, could only be defeated by
dethroning the demonic powers behind the Empire.

And the demonic powers could only be dethroned
by converting the humans who lent them their authority
and dominion. Satan has no authority, so he usurps
authority from humans through deception. Humans
believe his lies and hand over the keys to their house.
Jesus came to expose the lies, declare the truth and
bring humans back into the dominion-with-God camp.
Jesus came to recover the keys.

This means that the kingdom of God advances in
the earth by converting human hearts. Jesus said, "The
kingdom of God is within you" (Luke 17:21). Paul said
the kingdom is "righteousness, peace and joy in the
Holy Spirit" (Romans 14:17). The Powers are dethroned
when humans are converted and retract their authority
from their old alliance with evil. The contract with
death is cancelled, and the heart is transformed. The
kingdom of God does not come through violence, but
it comes through love.

Love liberates the heart.

The advance of Christ's kingdom through love
started when the Holy Spirit was poured out. The
church learned that the kingdom would not come
through military or political conquest. The kingdom
would come through the preaching of the gospel, the

Good News that Jesus rose from the dead and rules over all creation. That fact, when believed, breaks the lie of the Evil One and strips him of his power.

Love destroys the lie.

Love destroys the Liar.

The early church believed that the kingdom of God was meant to triumph in the earth *now*. Paul quoted Isaiah and declared, "Behold, now is the favorable time; behold, now is the day of salvation" (2 Corinthians 6:2). The day of Israel's salvation is *now*. Jesus is Israel's salvation. His resurrection guaranteed the resurrection of Israel and all creation with her. In fact, when Jesus arose, we all arose *in him*, which makes our resurrection at the last day inevitable.

The resurrection of Jesus drew the promised future back into the middle of history and inaugurated the kingdom of God here and now, releasing it to grow slowly but surely in every nation under heaven until all the Powers are subdued under Christ. Jesus called the kingdom of God "yeast" that would inexorably "leaven" the whole (Matthew 13:33).

The early church definitely believed that Jesus would return to earth. They believed in the Second Coming, and so must we. But they believed that the Second Coming was the completion of Christ's victory over the Powers, not its beginning.

As Hebrews puts it,

He sat down at the right hand of God, waiting from that time until his enemies should be made a footstool for his feet. (Hebrews 10:12–13)

Jesus rules *now* at the right hand of God "anticipating" the defeat of his enemies. As Paul said, Jesus rules "not only in this age, but also in the one to come." Take a moment to read Paul's full quote in Ephesians—it's worth your attention!

[God] raised [Jesus] from the dead and seated him at his right hand in the heavenly places, far above all rule and authority and power and dominion, and above every name that is named, not only in this age but also in the one to come. And he put all things under his feet and gave him as head over all things to the church, which is his body, the fullness of him who fills all in all. (Ephesians 1:20–23)

Did you get that? "Not only in this age, but also in the one to come." Paul's working assumption was that Jesus rules *now*. We must not postpone the rule of Jesus until after the Second Coming. He rules *now*.

In heaven, Jesus is exalted above the Powers. In heaven, "all things"—*ta panta*, Greek for "the universe"—are placed under Jesus' feet. It's an already-done fact. But don't miss the punchline: Jesus is Lord of all *through his church*. Jesus is "head over all things to the church, which is his body, the fullness of him who fills all in all."

The church is Jesus' body, and the church, as you probably know, is still on earth. (Quick! Check: are you still on Planet Earth? Good.) The rule of Jesus extends from heaven into earth through the church. Dominion flows from the head into the body. The head leads, the body follows.

And, through the church, Jesus executes his rule over all things. The church is the threshold of the kingdom. Through the church, people are baptized into Christ and enter the kingdom of God. The kingdom of God influences the world through love.

All things are brought to "fullness" (Gr. — *pleroma*) through Christ's headship over the church. He rules through his people and "fills all in all." Jesus works in partnership with the church to fill all things.

Jesus will "fill all things" (Ephesians 4:10), and he will do so through the church. Read Ephesians 4 carefully to get a better grasp of how Jesus will "fill all things." It happens through the church.

"The fullness of him who fills all in all" is dominion language. It is an echo of Genesis 1:28 where God told Adam and Eve to "fill the earth."

And God blessed them. And God said to them, "Be fruitful and multiply and fill the earth and subdue it, and have dominion over the fish of the sea and over the birds of the heavens and over every living thing that moves on the earth." (Genesis 1:28)

Jesus came to "fill all things." Jesus came to restore usurped human dominion. And it's happening *now.*

Look at Revelation 1:

John to the seven churches that are in Asia: Grace to you and peace from him who is and who was and who is to come, and from the seven spirits who are before his throne, and from Jesus Christ the faithful witness, the firstborn of the dead, and the ruler of kings on earth. To him who loves us and has freed us from our sins by his blood and made us a kingdom, priests to his God and Father, to him be glory and dominion forever and ever. Amen. (Revelation 1:4–6)

Jesus is "the ruler of kings on the earth." And he has "made us a kingdom." Jesus has "dominion forever and ever." Strong statements about the present reality of Christ's rule from heaven over earth.

The goal of history is to see heaven come to earth, to see his "kingdom come, [his] will be done, on earth as it is in heaven" (Matthew 6:10). Jesus told us to pray this now. We should no more postpone our hope for heaven on earth than we should postpone our hope for daily bread, forgiveness or deliverance from the Evil One—all powerful, right-now parts of the Lord's Prayer.

The game is a cosmic contest. It is a struggle for control of culture, for the future of the world. For the Powers, it is a fight to the death. They know that Christ's ultimate victory means their total destruction. So they fight with everything they've got. And God works for us as we pray *within that reality.* This means that sometimes prayers take time.

We all know God could snap his fingers and— BOOM!—the victory would be won. But God is not trying to win the victory for himself. He wants to win it through us so that *we* can be trained in what victory looks like and feels like. Just like me with my son's homework, God wants to train us for an ever-increasing glory. He wants you and me to overcome the Evil One. And this means that triumph takes time.

God works through *people,* and God works through *process.*

CHAPTER SIX

ANGELS

Here's another thing we should know about the process: God works through angels. He not only works within the reality of human freedom and demonic resistance, but he works through these amazing beings called "messengers" in the Bible. The picture isn't really complete until we talk about how God uses angels to support us in spiritual warfare.

If we are to "get in the game," then we need to recognize the support staff that stands behind us. Think coaches, trainers, medical staff—that's sort of what angels are to us. Which is pretty darn amazing, if you think about it.

By the way, there are countless wonderful books written on the ministry of angels, and I recommend you read them all. Sort through them with a Bible in your hand. There's so much to learn about angels, and our understanding is just getting started. Who knows, God may give you insights to share and you'll write the next book on angels.

One thing we know is that God administrates the universe through the ministry of angels. He governs nature, guides the stars, steers the planets, controls the seasons, releases the wind and manages the storms through angels. Numerous scriptures speak of the role of angels in God's sovereign administration over heaven and earth.

Of course, the world the angels govern is quite different from the world God created. Due to Adam's sin, the world now groans under the curse and will do so until the resurrection when "the creation itself will be set free from its bondage to corruption and obtain the freedom of the glory of the children of God" (Romans 8:21). In practical terms, this means that the powers of evil can interfere with the forces of nature and wreak havoc on the world.

Remember when Jesus calmed the storm? (Mark 4:35-5:20) He "rebuked" it—which means that the storm was driven by a demonic power. As Bill Johnson often says, if God had been the author of the storm, then Jesus' would have rebuked his own Father. And that's not likely. The storm was definitely driven by evil powers, by the demons that possessed the man in the tombs. They felt Jesus coming. No doubt, this happens often. So, when God uses angels to manage the weather, they do so against the real resistance of demonic forces.

When you see a hurricane, don't blame it on God. The earth is groaning under the curse, and natural disasters are the earth rocking and rolling with paroxysms of travail. The ground cries out against the evil staining its soil. (Genesis 4:10) The Bible says that the earth "vomits out its inhabitants" (Leviticus 15:25, 28). Nature itself reacts to evil.

But God reacts with love and sends deliverance to the land. See that FEMA trailer? Right beside the Red Cross tent? That's God working through people. That's people getting in the game.

The Father works against the devastation caused by natural disasters, for natural disasters are not natural at all. God did not make the world to be like this. The disorder we see around us is a result of the fall of man and the entrance of sin into God's good creation. And God will not leave it as it is—he plans to redeem it all.

However, remember—God works in the world *as it is*, not as we wish it was. He works against the forces of pain-convulsed, demon-driven nature by sending his angels into the storm. He speaks the word and the storm is calmed. Angels are "mighty ones who do his word, obeying the voice of his word!" (Psalm 103:20)

Yet, here's the kicker: God speaks his word through *us*. As Jesus told us, the mountain moves when *we* speak to the mountain. Same with storms. When God gets ready to speak peace into a storm, he will speak through us.

That's a shocker. In fact, most Christians do not believe we have a role to play in calming storms. When was the last time we heard of anyone standing with authority and commanding a storm to stop? Think of what would happen if Christians everywhere really believed that we have power to release holy angels into the forces of nature and bend the wind to the will of the Father. Think what would happen if we joined forces in prayer to calm the forces of nature.

I think the church is awakening to her role in affecting nature. You talk about the ultimate, God-centered environmentalism! When the church awakens to her role in stewarding creation, we will muster our prayers to bring creation itself back under the dominion of redeemed humanity through the limitless power of the Holy Spirit.

Jesus didn't calm the storm just to show us what he could do. Of course, he can calm the storm—he's God. But he did not calm the storm as God; he calmed the storm as a God-filled-man. And, as a man, he showed us what humans filled with the Spirit of God can do in the world.

Jesus promised that we would do "greater works" than he did while on earth.

Truly, truly, I say to you, whoever believes in me will also do the works that I do; and greater works than these will he do, because I am going to the Father. Whatever you ask in my name, this I will do, that the Father may be glorified in the Son. If you ask me anything in my name, I will do it. (John 14:12–14)

The "greater works" include taking dominion over creation. The "greater works" include calming the storm.

Watch and see what God will do: the church is awakening to the mighty power we have. The next few generations are going to see an increase of dramatic miracles over nature itself. Droughts will be broken. Famines will end. Pestilence will vanish. Wildfires will be extinguished. Cancer will be eradicated. Diabetes will be a faint memory. And all of this will happen through a blend of the "natural" and "supernatural" (as we tend to describe what we can do and what God can do).

• Scientists and medical researchers will discover by the power of the Holy Spirit how to create cures that will heal sickness all around the world.

• Engineers inspired by "spiritual intelligence" (as Kris Vallotton describes it) will discover new ways to mine resources without harming the planet, new ways to get water to parched deserts, new ways to build sustainable housing in the poorest parts of the world.

• Economists informed by kingdom values will shift financial and monetary policy so that the wealth of nations will benefit the poorest among us.

• Technologists will continue to push the frontiers of computer science and harness the quantum power latent within God's good creation.

• Statesmen/women and politicians will negotiate peace that makes war a long-forgotten horror from our barbaric past. Nations will practice statecraft and diplomacy rather than warcraft and destruction.

Miracles will happen in the most ordinary ways. Like water becoming wine. All of it through *process*. All of it through *partnership* with God. When humans wake up to the limitless, infinite power available to us, the world will become a different place. And it's happening now. Watch and see. It can't help but happen, for Jesus is Lord.

All through partnership with God. And partnership with God means partnership with angels. All through Scripture, we see example after example of God working with and through angels.

In the Old Covenant era, angels were like palace guardians who trained the sons and daughters of the

King. Tutors and governors, Paul called them. (Galatians 4:1) In the New Covenant era, the sons and daughters of the King are grown up in Christ and rule together with the Father.

(See Galatians 4 and Hebrews 1, 2 for great teaching on angels as guardians and intermediaries under the Law of Moses.)

Angels were created to assist us in our role as God's regent rulers over all creation. Angels were created to help us exercise dominion over the world.

Are [angels] not all ministering spirits sent out to serve for the sake of those who are to inherit salvation? (Hebrews 1:14)

Angels were created to serve those who "inherit salvation," which is a much bigger concept than just "going to heaven when we die." Salvation in the Bible is comprehensive. It includes our individual and personal salvation, for sure; but it also includes the salvation of all creation, the redemption of the planet and eradication of evil from God's good world. Salvation includes dominion. Angels serve that divine-human agenda.

(Start with N.T. Wright, *Surprised By Hope* to get a good introduction to the broader idea of salvation.)

God works through angels, and angels work with us. Yet many Christians are not fully aware of the role that angels play in our dominion and in spiritual warfare. The work cannot be done without them. Because we wrestle with Powers we cannot see, angels we cannot see (usually) are essential to our task.

Angels are assigned to serve us. Angels are messengers, warriors and worshippers. They ascend and descend continually upon the body of Christ between heaven and earth. (Genesis 28:12; John 1:51) After the Holy Spirit was poured out at Pentecost, the ministry of angels dramatically increased in the world, as the Book of Acts shows. To put it bluntly, we cannot do what Jesus called us to do without angels.

Obviously—though Paul still needed to say so!—we should not worship angels. (Colossians 2:18) But neither should we ricochet into the opposite error of ignoring them. We should work to better understand the ministry of angels and release them with our dominion decree into the world we are called to rule by serving in love.

I remember a prayer gathering at my house once where I saw a mental image while we prayed. It felt like I was lifted up about a thousand feet above our house. Like hovering in a helicopter. Down below, I saw a grayish, whitish column spinning over our house. About fifty feet across and two or three hundred feet tall. It was not a funnel cloud like a tornado, but it was as wide at the base as it was at the top. Straight up and down like a Greek column, but spinning. And it was hollow in the middle, creating an opening through the middle between our house and heaven. Like a pipeline.

Then, as I looked closer, I saw that the walls of the circling column were made up of angels ascending and descending over our house as we prayed. The grayish-whitish color of the column was actually the wings of the angels reflecting the evening sun. Like a bank of clouds after a storm. The column was a spiral that spun higher and higher as the angels ascended, while another stream of angels descended in the opposite direction. Our prayers created an open heaven, and the spiral cloud of angels moved into the space and moved up and down on our prayers.

It was amazing.

Another experience of seeing angels happened in the early summer of 2014. I was asleep, middle of the night, when I was lifted in a dream through the ceiling of our bedroom. Our bedroom has a two-tiered recessed ceiling, and a ceiling fan hangs in the middle. I was lifted through the ceiling center as if it were an open skylight.

I emerged through the ceiling onto the edge of a large meadow. About a thousand yards across the meadow was a line of trees in the distance, gray and hazy with mist, as if the morning sun was just about to rise. Felt quite early, predawn.

As I looked across the meadow, I realized I was standing on the edge, along the sideline, of a great battlefield. To my right, gathering in the distant haze was an army of angels. They formed a massive line that stretched the full width of the meadow and extended rows and rows deep, farther than I could see.

Then, to my left, maybe five hundred yards away, I saw a dark, shadowy mass of creatures, indistinct and menacing. I did not see the figures in this mass as clearly as I saw the ranks of angels to my right, but I knew without hesitation that this was a demon horde, an army of evil spirits.

It was like a scene from *Lord of the Rings*. The holy angel army lifted up a roar that shook the ground and charged forward into the writhing, twisting mass of screaming demons. The dark army fell back in disarray, and the holy angels drove through them triumphantly and scattered them from the field of battle.

I can still hear the clashing of armor, the clanging of swords, the roar of the warriors. I can still feel the heat, though I was not burned. I can still smell the acrid, stinging smoke of the battle. It was *so* real to me.

In the next moment, I was back in my bed, still asleep, but fully alert in my dream. I was lying in bed looking up at the ceiling, when I saw two angels peering down through the skylight-like opening in the recess. All I could see was their faces staring down at me like two kids looking over the rail of a mezzanine at the mall. They looked mostly curious. It was like they had to come see exactly for whom they were fighting.

I am not sure they were all that impressed.

But, seriously, it did seem like they were quite curious, almost childlike in their wonder toward me. I can still see the scene right now, clear as a bell, in my head.

Talk about angels in the ceiling. My own Sistine Chapel.

I jolted awake, and the Lord God said to me— again, clear as a bell, almost audibly: "I am fighting your battles for you." And that was it.

I sat up on the edge of the bed and replayed what I had seen. It was breathtaking. It left me stunned, speechless, humbled beyond words to consider how much the God of heaven cared for me.

I'll tell you more of the story soon, but Jeana and I, along with many friends in the church we led at the time, were embarking on the most dangerous transition we had ever undertaken by leaving our lifelong tradition, the Oneness Pentecostal movement. And, as it turned out, it was a long, slow walk through hell.

Satan did everything in his power for the next five years to utterly take us out of the game. There's no way to exaggerate how traumatic it was.

But I never forgot the vision of holy angels fighting the battle for me. Never forgot the bemused faces of those two guardians sent to escort us safely through the wilderness. Never forgot the word of the Lord, "I am fighting your battles for you."

In fact, I saw them again not long ago, the same two angels. This time, they appeared as two professional divers wearing ball caps—I kid you not!—dressed all in black, sitting with me in a small aluminum boat about to plunge to the depths of some unknown body of water. I was scared and too proud to admit it. One of them turned back to me to help me with my diving equipment (as I pretended to know what I was doing!), and his easy smile and "Aw, shucks" manner reassured me that these two guys did actually know exactly what they were doing, and that they would not let anything bad happen to me.

It was one of the most peace-giving experiences I've ever had.

Here's the point: God works in the world *as it is* through the agency of angels. Angels ascend and descend between heaven and earth ministering to the children of God. They fight our battles. They guide and guard us through difficult times. They minister strength when we are weak.

Worshipping angels stand before the throne of God crying, "Holy, holy holy, Lord God Almighty!" They also gather with us when we worship and join the chorus of praise. We may not see them on Sunday—or whenever we gather in the name of Jesus—but our assembly includes "innumerable angels in festal gathering" (Hebrews 12:22).

Messenger angels carry dispatches from earth to heaven and from heaven to earth. They also deliver parcels of healing, nourishment and strength to the spiritually exhausted. Messenger angels respond to the prayers of the saints and bring key directives to those who are alert to their ministry. The angel that spoke with Cornelius is a prime example. (Acts 10:1-8) There are numerous others.

Then, there are the warrior angels, the angels who fight on our behalf. These are the heavenly hosts who drive back the powers of evil. In fact, God is called "the Lord of Armies" due to how he works through the ministry of warring angels.

And those three types of angels only scratch the surface of the myriad creatures God formed to display his glory and serve his mission. Cherubim, seraphim, sons of God, elohim, watchers, guardian angels, on and on it goes.

Yet the main thing that matters to our "get in the game" exhortation is that *angels minister for us in the world as it is, not as we wish it was.* In other words, holy angels are not all-powerful gods who can just zap their opponents, dust off their hands and go to the house. There is a real battle being fought every day for heavenly and earthly dominion.

Just like the vision I saw in my ceiling—and just like the incredible battle scenes depicted in *Lord of the Rings*—the battle is intense, real and fought hard to the bitter end. And get this: the immediate outcome is not pre-determined. Yes, we are guaranteed the *final outcome: we win.* But that doesn't mean that every skirmish ends with good triumphing over evil. Sometimes evil wins.

The triumph of good over evil takes time. The battle must be fought and won in the arena of human decision, demonic resistance and angelic warfare.

This is why we must not lose heart when answers are delayed. Keep praying. Keep fasting. Keep declaring the promises of God. Keep speaking faith in the face of every loss. Keep pressing forward in relentless determination.

Stay in the game!

Get this—I keep saying this to drive the point home: God works in the world *as it is*, not as we wish it was.

I keep saying this because too often we think God will just snap his fingers and—BAM!—the work will be done, the prayer will be answered, the miracle will happen. And that happens sometimes, no doubt. But more often than not, miracles take time. And they take time because God works out his will in the world through people and through process. And the process involves spiritual warfare.

CHAPTER SEVEN

THE STORY OF DANIEL

The story of Daniel is one of the best examples of how God works in the real world as it is. Specifically, *The Book of Daniel*, Chapter 10. Take a moment to read the entire chapter for full context.

Wait a second. Just before you read the chapter, we need quick disclaimer about Danielic relevance. (I just made that word up out of thin air; but I really like it, so we're going with it. *Danielic.* Very good.)

*Disclaimer on Danielic Relevance: As you may know, Daniel's story is an Old Covenant story, lived and told long before the death and resurrection of Jesus. Some may be tempted to believe, then, that the battle described in Daniel 10 is a spiritual reality rendered obsolete by the cross of Jesus and no longer relevant to the New Covenant era. Some believe that the defeat of the Powers at the cross rendered them null and void ever since. Some even believe that the Powers were banished to Tartarus and no longer function in the world at all.

Obviously, I don't agree.

I think I addressed fairly well above that there is an ongoing battle with the Powers, but I want to make sure going into Daniel 10 that we appreciate this ancient prophecy as relevant to today's spiritual warfare.

One clear interpretive signal that Daniel's work foretells the New Covenant era is that the major themes of *Daniel are* woven throughout the *Book of Revelation,* which is written to a New Covenant audience. Countless prophetic scholars have shown how *Revelation* echoes *Daniel.*

Indeed, *Revelation* is presented by John as the fulfillment of the Danielic prophecies postponed by Israel's unbelief. As the angel said, "Go your way, Daniel, for the words are shut up and sealed until the time of the end" (Daniel 12:9). In *Revelation,* "the time is near" (Revelation 1:3; 22:10), and the seals placed on Daniel's prophecies are broken off one-by-one until all is fulfilled. (Revelation 5-8)

Regardless of whether you see *Revelation* from the historicist, futurist, preterist or idealist point of view, its fulfillment lies on this side of Calvary, placed squarely within the New Covenant age.

The battle described in John's vision on Patmos is a ongoing battle until Jesus returns in the Second Coming. This aligns perfectly with 1 Corinthians 15 where, as we saw above, the subduing of Christ's enemies continues until "the end" when Jesus returns and defeats Death, the "last enemy." Yes, Christ is Victor, but *Christus Victor* still rides out to make war.

> *Then I saw heaven opened, and behold, a white horse! The one sitting on it is called Faithful and True, and in righteousness he judges and makes war. His eyes are like a flame of fire, and on his head are many diadems, and he has a name written that no one knows but himself. He is clothed in a robe dipped in blood, and the name by which he is called is The Word of God.*

> *And the armies of heaven, arrayed in fine linen, white and pure, were following him on white horses. From his mouth comes a sharp sword with which to strike down the nations, and he will rule them with a rod of iron. He will tread the winepress of the fury of the wrath of God the Almighty. On his robe and on his thigh he has a name written, King of kings and Lord of lords. (Revelation 19:11–16)*

In *Revelation,* the battle between good and evil is still being played out on the field of human history, between the First and Second Advents of Christ. That's right now.

Therefore, the *Book of Revelation* pulls the *Book of Daniel* right smack dab in the middle of the New Covenant era. Ergo, we can read Daniel 10 as a description of what we face today in spiritual warfare. And that's the main point for now.

*End of Disclaimer. Now, you are okay to go back and read the full context of Daniel 10.

Here's the money quote:

Then he said to me, "Fear not, Daniel, for from the first day that you set your heart to understand and humbled yourself before your God, your words have been heard, and I have come because of your words.

The prince of the kingdom of Persia withstood me twenty-one days, but Michael, one of the chief princes, came to help me, for I was left there with the kings of Persia, and came to make you understand what is to happen to your people in the latter days. For the vision is for days yet to come." (Daniel 10:12–14)

Daniel fasted and prayed for twenty-one days seeking answers regarding prophetic visions he had received. Three weeks of fervent prayer, yet no answer. Somehow, Daniel had the gumption, as my dad would've said, to keep praying, believing that the answer would eventually come. And it did: twenty-one days later.

Daniel's endurance was remarkable. But what is even more remarkable is the backstory on what took so long. The angel, Gabriel, spilled the tea, as my kids would say. He gave Daniel the gist.

From day one, Daniel's prayer had been heard, and Gabriel left heaven to bring Daniel his answer. But a funny thing happened on the way to Daniel's house: Gabriel ran into a spiritual blockade. The Prince of Persia, one of the Powers we talked about earlier, "withstood" Gabriel twenty-one days.

Michael, "one of the chief princes," an archangel, as some describe him, and also the Prince assigned to the Nation of Israel, came to help Gabriel and delivered him from the nasty Prince of Persia. Gabriel, now free from the demonic blockade, streaked across the sky like lightning and landed at Daniel's house.

Now, every element of "the game" we've discussed so far in this short book is present in this story. God is here, for it is he who sends Gabriel to Daniel's house. The angels are here, Michael, Gabriel and countless others, surely, left unnamed. And there go the Powers, the fallen angels who resist God's will.

And standing at the center of it all is a human, a frail, fickle, frightened human. Daniel is the central character in the story, for everything hinges on him. What if Daniel gives up? What happens if he get exhausted and walks off the field? What happens if Daniel refuses to get in the game? Or stay in the game?

Look again at what the angel said to Daniel:

"Fear not, Daniel, for from the first day that you set your heart to understand and humbled yourself before your God, your words have been heard, and I have come because of your words.

(1) "Fear not, Daniel." Daniel was scared, but he was determined to get an answer. Daniel refused to avoid the issue and retreat into nihilistic despair. Daniel refused to embrace a cynical, *whatever* attitude. He was afraid, but he insisted on getting in the game.

(2) "From the day that you set your heart to understand and humbled yourself before your God." Daniel moved heaven from day one. God was not holding out on him. The delay in Daniel's answer was not due to God's reluctance. God was eager to answer, but God works in the world *as it is,* not as we wish it was.

(3) Daniel "set [his] heart to understand." Daniel was *determined.* His heart was "set" (fixed) on getting an answer. What is your heart set on? Are you willing to persevere in prayer when answers are delayed? It takes determination to get in the game and stay there.

(4) And—here's the kicker!—"Your *words* have been heard, and I have come because of your

words." We will talk more about this in a moment, but your *words* are the single greatest way you get in the game. You get in the game primarily through *prayer, praise* and *prophecy* (declaring the words of God over your life). Your words summon angels with answers, but you must keep on making war with words until the Powers are pushed back by angels armies and the answer comes.

Now, the scene in Daniel 10 is hugely important because this is how the purpose of God gets done in the earth. There is war in heaven, and the prayers of the saints shift the outcome. The battle rages in the heavens as the armies of holy angels break through the phalanx of demons who withstand God's will. And the battle is *real*. It's not a charade played on stage for dramatic effect. The Powers really do resist. They do "withstand" holy angels as they go forth to serve the heirs of salvation.

Remember this when you struggle to keep on praying. Remember this when you are tempted to give up. You have a role to play. The angels are battling on your behalf, and they need you to just keep believing. They need you to get in the game.

CHAPTER EIGHT

THE NEXT BIG THING

Now, we've covered a lot of ground since we started off with Doris Day singing, *Que Sera, Sera*. We shushed dear Doris and told her firmly but kindly that we refuse to accept the *whatever will be, will be* nonsense. No way. We believe that we have a role to play in the game of life. We are *not* victims.

Next, we took careful aim at two stubborn myths: (1) that we are just spectators in the game of life; and (2) that God always works instantly when he works at all. We proceeded to blow those two myths to sky-high smithereens by looking at how God works through *people* and through *process*.

In the *people* section, we saw that the heavens belong to the Lord, but the earth belongs to humans. We opined briefly that God respects freedom because he is love, and he respects authority because he is just. God moves in the world only as people invite him. He still stands at the door and knocks.

Then, we took a deep dive into how God works through *process*. And this is where it got really good.

We declared—over and over, in fact—that God works through the world *as it is,* rather than as we wish it was. We saw how God works within the permission and cooperation of human freedom; against real demonic resistance, particularly the Powers; and through the agency of holy angels.

If you missed any of that, head back up front and reread the relevant pages.

The key point in all of this is to show that the game is real. Actually, the game is not a game at all; it is deadly serious. Yet, the "game" metaphor works really well when boldly awakening believers to get involved in the outcome of unpredictable life-situations. The game is real, and the immediate outcome is unclear. For we have a role to play in how the game plays out.

How we view our role in the game will largely be determined by our view of God's sovereignty. I spent several years arcing widely through the distant realms of Reformed Theology before I boomeranged back to a more "synergistic" view of God's work in the world. My roots are in Pentecostal theology, which is more "Arminian" than Reformed, if you know what all that means. If not, Google it and be prepared for a wild ride through hotly contested territory.

(Read D. A. Carson, *Divine Sovereignty and Human Responsibility* for a good Reformed overview, and

Roger Olson, *Against Calvinism* for a good Arminian overview.)

Be that as it may, I wrestled powerfully for years with the idea of God's sovereignty. And, for me, it seems that the best witness of Scripture is that God sovereignly chose to work through the free decision of humans, through a free will liberated by grace and empowered to cooperate with the active, life-changing Spirit of God.

And we've waded through all the obscure theological jargon to get at this point: too many people blame bad situations on "the will of God." And it's gotta stop.

Bad thing happens: "Welp, it musta been the will of God! Nothing really anyone could do about it." And we slouch our way home "tsk, tsk-ing" all the way.

Then, to make it worse, we pietize (another excellent made-up word meaning "to make things seem pious") bad outcomes and call it "suffering for the name of Jesus." The bad part is that there really *is* a time to suffer for his name—when we're being persecuted, for example. But even then, persecution is ironically designed to subvert the power of the enemy and defeat suffering by absorbing, redeeming and overthrowing it. Even when we're meant to suffer, it is for the larger purpose of glory and transformation. In the kingdom, suffering ends. And it ends in glory.

(The apostle Peter wrote a entire book on the topic of redemptive suffering, *The First Epistle of Peter,* in the New Testament. Check it out when you have a moment. Fantastic read!)

All redemptive suffering leads to glory, which means we must discard theologies that enshrine defeat as a Christian virtue. Too many Christians define Christianity only by the cross, and wear the emblem of suffering to excuse a tacit surrender to the enemy. Heads bowed, hands clasped, pitiful, defeated Christians. In reality, our faith is defined more by the resurrection than it is by the cross. The cross has no one on it. Jesus arose.

The cross alone could never save us. It was the resurrection of Jesus—his triumph over the Powers—that made the cross effective. If Jesus hadn't risen from the dead, the cross would have been just another long-forgotten Roman execution.

Paul the apostle declared that, without the resurrection, "our preaching is in vain and your faith is in vain" (1 Corinthians 15:14). Without the resurrection, "your faith is futile and you are still in your sins" (1 Corinthians 15:17). The preaching of the cross without the resurrection would make us "of all people most to be pitied" (1 Corinthians 15:19).

When you decided to become a Christian, you were called to "take up your cross" and follow Jesus. (Matthew 16:24) But follow to *where?* To the cross, yes. But Jesus didn't stay on the cross. He was buried and rose again. Then, he ascended to heaven and was seated on the throne of God. And *that* is exactly where you are called to follow.

You are crucified with Christ, yes. But you do not stay there. You are buried with him, and you rise with him. Then—and don't miss this part!—you ascend with Jesus and you are seated "with him in the heavenly places in Christ Jesus" (Ephesians 2:6).

Too many of us are willing to die with Jesus, but we refuse to reign with him. *We don't want the responsibility.* We are afraid we will fail, so we climb back on the cross and play it safe by doing non-stop penance, pretending to be humble when in reality we are just afraid.

We create theologies of suffering to excuse our abdication of responsibility. Or, worst of all, we develop doctrines (like cessationism) that entrench unbelief by arguing that the age of miracles is over and God doesn't supernaturally intervene like that anymore.

(Think about it: *as if* we can encounter God—the supernatural God!—without seeing miracles. That's like touching an exposed electrical wire without getting shocked. God is by definition supernatural, and we should expect nothing less than the supernatural when encountering him.)

We also, to avoid responsibility, create eschatologies (doctrines on the end of the world) that postpone the victory of Jesus until after the Second Coming. We bunker down in our churches praying for Jesus to come back and do what he told *us* to do. We reassure ourselves that only the return of Christ can fix the world's problems.

But the answer to the world's problems is you. More broadly, it is a Spirit-filled, Spirit-led church. Which includes you. God dreamed that up. There is no Plan B. God's solution is *people* and *process*. That's what the church is all about.

The church is the threshold of the kingdom, and the kingdom encompasses every realm of life. The kingdom of God is like yeast in the dough (Matthew 13, again), and it is designed to influence everything it touches for good. The kingdom influences your work. The kingdom influences your neighborhood. Your school. Your government. Your bowling alley. *Everything is influenced by the kingdom!*

As Abraham Kuyper famously said, "There is not a square inch in the whole domain of our human existence over which Christ, who is Sovereign over all, does not cry: 'Mine!" The Moravians launched the world's greatest missions movement with the cry, "May the Lamb that was slain receive the reward of his suffering!"

The Lord Jesus purchased everything with his blood. All of it. The Father promised Jesus the entire world:

The Lord said to me, "You are my Son; today I have begotten you. Ask of me, and I will make the nations your heritage, and the ends of the earth your possession. (Psalm 2:7–8)

But the really important fact is that Jesus was promised the earth as his inheritance *as the son of man —a human.* Jesus will receive his inheritance in and through us. This is why Jesus quoted Psalm 2 when he commissioned the apostles as "witnesses...to the ends of the earth" (Acts 1:8). Jesus will receive his inheritance of all nations through the ever-expanding witness of the church in the earth.

The promise of inheritance that Jesus received from the Father was an echo of the promise made to Abraham that all the nations of the earth would be blessed through his offspring. (Genesis 12:1-3) Jesus is the singular "Offspring of Abraham" (Galatians 3:16), and, as the heir of Abraham, Jesus inherited the world. Abraham believed the promise that "he would be heir of the world" (Romans 4:13), and Jesus received what Abraham believed.

In fact, Jesus is *still receiving through us* what Abraham believed. We "walk in the footsteps of the faith that our father Abraham had" (Romans 4:12) when we walk out our faith in the world. When two or three believers gather in the name of Jesus, Jesus is there. We take Jesus into the nations. We are his hands and feet.

God so loved the world (the "cosmos") that he gave his Son. (John 3:16) God loves his good creation, and he plans to redeem it. He is "making all things new" (Revelation 21:5). Jesus told us, "Go into all the world ("cosmos" again) and proclaim the gospel to the whole creation" (Mark 16:15). *The whole creation.* Did you get that? Our commission is to preach the good news to *the whole creation.* Not just the human population within creation.

And the good news for the whole creation is that the resurrection of Jesus brought the future into the present, and the work of new creation has already begun. And—here we go again!—the way that old creation becomes new creation is through *people* and *process,* through saved people mediating new creation into the world via redeemed dominion.

Look at 2 Corinthians 5:

Therefore, if anyone is in Christ, he is a new creation. The old has passed away; behold, the new has come. All this is from God, who through Christ reconciled us to himself and gave us the ministry of reconciliation; that is, in Christ God was reconciling the world to himself, not counting their trespasses against them, and entrusting to us the message of reconciliation. (2 Corinthians 5:17–19)

As N. T Wright likes to point out, Paul's original phrasing actually says, "Therefore, if anyone is in Christ—new creation!" In other words, the "new creation" here is not referring only to how one person is made new, to an *individual new creation*. No, the fact that individuals are a new creation means that the *cosmic new creation* has come. The new creation foretold by the prophets is already present in the world, and regenerated people are the proof of that.

Because *you* are saved, the world will be saved. Changed people change the world. Through you and me, the reconciliation of *all things* is guaranteed. God is "entrusting to us the message of reconciliation." The message of reconciliation that we preach—that everything is *already reconciled* to God in Christ— mediates and manifests actualized reconciliation all over the planet.

Again, God completes the work through *people* and *process*. God "gave us the ministry of reconciliation," so the redemption of our Father's world happens gradually but inexorably through us. The full scope of our mission is global; indeed, it's universal. All creation shall be made new through the new birth.

And the salvation of all creation will be fully and finally complete when Jesus returns after subduing his enemies under his feet (1 Corinthians 15, again). When Jesus returns,

> *[He] will descend from heaven with a cry of command, with the voice of an archangel, and with the sound of the trumpet of God. And the dead in Christ will rise first.*
>
> *Then we who are alive, who are left, will be caught up together with them in the clouds to meet the Lord in the air, and so we will always be with the Lord. (1 Thessalonians 4:16–17)*

When Jesus raises the dead at the Second Coming, all creation will be raised from the dead. Creation will be "born again," made new forever. As Paul said,

> *The creation itself will be set free from its bondage to corruption and obtain the freedom of the glory of the children of God. (Romans 8:21)*

And that final work of resurrection has already begun in us *now*. (Ephesians 2:1) That's what the resurrection of Jesus did: he brought "the powers of the age to come" (Hebrews 6:5) into the middle of human history so that humans could be partners with God in the work of redemption.

Jesus guaranteed the resurrection of all things by sowing the seeds of resurrection within us through the Holy Spirit. And by indwelling us, Jesus ensured that his work will get done. *He is doing the work in us!*

Jesus, the "firstborn of creation" (Colossians 1:15) became the "firstborn from the dead" (Colossians 1:18) so we could be made new. And through us, all creation will be made new.

This is breathtaking. Indeed, many Christians struggle to grasp the full scope of redemption. We have been trained to postpone the big stuff until Jesus comes again. For many, the Rapture is the Next Big Thing. But Paul taught that "the fullness of the Gentiles" precipitating the salvation of Israel is the Next Big Thing:

> *Lest you be wise in your own sight, I do not want you to be unaware of this mystery, brothers: a partial hardening has come upon Israel, until the fullness of the Gentiles has come in. And in this way all Israel will be saved, as it is written, "The Deliverer will come from Zion, he will banish ungodliness from Jacob"; "and this will be my covenant with them when I take away their sins." (Romans 11:25).*

(The "fullness of the Gentiles" is what Isaiah prophesied about the pagan nations turning to Christ. Read Isaiah 42 for a glimpse of the exhilarating details. Or, if you want more, read all of Isaiah. It will set your sanctified imagination on fire!)

We are called the preach the gospel of the kingdom until "the earth [is] filled with the knowledge of the glory of the Lord as the waters cover the sea" (Habakkuk 2:14). We are called to live out the international blessing of Abraham until ethnic Jews are provoked to jealousy and their hearts miraculously turn back to Christ as their Messiah. (Romans 11:11)

Jews and Gentiles gathered together once more in the unified body of Christ and resurrected together at the last day with all creation is the full scope of redemption. (Ephesians 2:11-3:13) That's the "fullness" (Gr. — *pleroma*) that Paul keeps talking about. And the reunion of the divided church will be the catalyst of the End, the signal for the Grand Finale of human history and the return of our Lord when "all things" will be made new.

All that "fullness" talk requires another book. I may call it, *The Next Big Thing*. That sounds fun.

Anyhow, we manufacture theologies and eschatologies to avoid the full implications of the Great Commission. We shrink back from the task due to limited faith; and then, we shrink the mission to fit our faith so we can feel faithful. We create these false theologies and eschatologies because we are afraid. We fear failure. We are afraid that we will not have what it takes to get the job done, to win the game.

The power of evil in the world can be overwhelming. Christ's victory is hard to see in a fallen world. It feels much better to pray for Christ's return than to engage a hostile culture and bring wise solutions to intractable, generational problems. It seems so hopeless. It's easy to believe that Jesus can return and kick the devil's behiney. But we are not so sure we can.

Getting in the game requires bold, irrational faith. We know Jesus can "heal the sick, raise the dead, cleanse lepers, cast out demons" (Matthew 10:8), but we are not sure *we* can. The problem is, Jesus told *us* to do these things. Read it again: the statement just quoted from Matthew 10 was an instruction from Jesus *for us*. And we must have faith to believe that Jesus will only command us to do what he will give us grace to do.

We must stop masking fear with religious platitudes. We must stop retreating under the bleachers, avoiding our God-given responsibility to change the world. We must get in the game.

What do you see wrong with the world? Drugs?
Human trafficking? Corrupt politics? War in the Middle
East? Domestic and international terrorism? Religious
fundamentalism? Hunger? Homelessness? Income
inequity? Slavery? Oppression of women and
minorities? Abuse of children and the elderly?
Wildfires? Hurricanes? Climate change? Overflowing
landfills? Oceans of plastic? Loss of personal freedom?
Abortion? Mass shootings? Tyrannical governments?
Pornography? Immorality? Wall St. corruption?
Oppressive tax policy? Injustice? Racism?

Did I miss any? Here's a blank to write in more:

_____

Or are your problems with the world closer to
home? Are you facing a financial crisis? A relationship
gone sour? Children run amuck? Devastating medical
diagnosis? Recurring depression? Emotional trauma?
Betrayal? Bitterness? Molested as a child? Raped by a
boyfriend? Bankruptcy? PTSD? Gut-wrenching church
split? Failure of a trusted spiritual leader? Lied on,
slandered, stabbed in the back? Panic attacks?
Unfaithful partner?

Again, did I miss any? Here's a blank to write in
more:

_____

I'm not being flippant. Seriously, write it down. (Since you're most likely reading a digital book, write it on the palm of your hand. Or a post-it note. But write it down!) You *must* identify the thing that's most wrong with your world, the thing that keeps you up at night, the thing that scares you rigid. Write it down.

Then, once you've written it down, face it. Summon your deepest courage. Draw hard on the faith of Jesus Christ within you and *face it*. You are not a victim. You are not helpless. You can do something about what you're facing or what you've been through. There are remedies hidden in Christ for every situation you face.

If your most pressing problems are the "big world" problems listed above, then explore creative ways to help solve the problems. Support a non-profit, or create your own. Run for office. Finish your degree. Learn a second language, become a translator. Paint over graffiti. Mow a grandma's grass. Go on a Daniel Fast. Volunteer for global missions. Tithe to your local church. Raise money for wells in Africa. March in the streets—peacefully, of course. Become a counselor at a women's center. Become a foster family. Adopt an orphaned child. Open doors for strangers. Intercede daily, make war in prayer. Worship wildly.

Have a better idea? Great. Now, do it. *Do something*. But don't just stand by and lament the sad state of the world. God so loved the world that he gave his Son—and he gave his Son to you so that, through you, his Son could save the world. The solutions to the world's problems are *in you*.

But you gotta get in the game.

Too many Christians sit on the sidelines because they are afraid. And many are afraid because of past disappointments. They just don't want to be let down again. They tried and failed (they think), so they are afraid to try again.

In fact, many Christians are paralyzed by a "spirit of disappointment." They not just ordinarily disappointed. They live under a soul crushing, mind-numbing spirit of disappointment, a demonic oppression designed to trap them in a never-ending cycle of inaction.

In the name of Jesus, we break that spirit of disappointment right now. Say these words with me right now. Stand up, put your hands high in the air, and say these words:

Father, in the name of Jesus, I surrender to you this spirit of disappointment. Father, I look back through the Holy Spirit to the time when I cast away my confidence, when I surrendered my faith to disappointment. I repent for believing that disappointment was the final word in my situation. Forgive me, Lord Jesus, for partnering with the lie that you could not be trusted. I renounce this demonic lie, in Jesus' name!

Father, release fresh hope in me now. Break the spirit of despair, annul my covenant with hopelessness, shatter the mindset of unbelief. Savior, deliver me! Break off every evil spirit that has attached to my mind. Set me free. In Jesus' name, I claim the victory that belongs to Christ. It is mine by birthright. I lay claim to my inheritance of overcoming faith. From this day forward, I will refuse to partner with the spirit of disappointment. In Jesus' name, it is done. Amen.

CONCLUSION

LET'S WRAP IT UP, DARN IT

O kay. Let's wrap it up. If I don't find a stopping place, this small book will grow pretentious and think it's full grown literature. Can't have that.

So, musicians come, and let's close this thing. I'll wrap it up like this:

We must be absolutely relentless. We must forcefully renounce our passive view of the will of God, as if we are observers watching the outcome. The will of God doesn't happen *to us*; the will of God happens *with us, for us* and *through us*. You have a role to play, so play it.

God is always reaching for greater things. It is his nature to increase. It is his nature to grow. Of course, God himself cannot get greater, but his works can. The revelation of who he is can. And does. As Isaiah said,

Of the increase of his government and of peace there will be no end, on the throne of David and over his kingdom, to establish it and to uphold it with justice and with righteousness from this time

forth and forevermore. The zeal of the Lord of hosts will do this. (Isaiah 9:7)

The government of God—Jesus called it "the kingdom of God"—will never stop growing. God is a *reacher*. Long before Jack. (Sorry, dad joke.) We must be *reachers*. We must pursue spectacular victory in the real world. We must remember what prayer really is: it is a human invitation for divine intervention. And we should expect divine intervention to be nothing less than spectacular.

If all we want is an ordinary solution, then why pray? Why not just sort it out for ourselves? But when we pray, we are opening the door to the supernatural. *That's why we pray!*

For many Christians, prayer is just a required religious ritual where we let God know what we plan to do today and ask for his approval. "Father God, we humbly beseech thee that thou wouldest nod thy holy head ever so slightly in our direction and signal thy kind approval for thy humble servant to do what he'd already planned to do without you."

Shucks.

Darn FYI prayers.

No way.

That's *not* what prayer is. Prayer is war. Prayer is calling in the artillery. Prayer is a divine summons for holy angels to explode out of heaven's gates armed to the teeth, ready for sensational, spectacular, earth-shaking battle. Nations will rise and fall as we pray. Presidents and Prime Ministers will rise and fall as we pray. Dictators will be overthrown. Governments will topple. Armies will flee in disarray. Financial markets will tremor and shake, the rich become poor and the poor become rich. All because we prayed, and the Powers of heaven were shaken.

Jeana once told me about a seasoned prayer warrior, way up in her eighties, who told of praying each morning based on the day's headlines. She would get up early, make a cup of coffee and watch the morning news shows. She would make notes as she watched, and then she would go to war in prayer over all the events happening around the world and around her city. That's getting in the game!

Recently, I've noticed a trend on social media. When tragedy strikes, especially school shootings, people often indignantly protest against expressions of sympathy by politicians and religious leaders: "We don't need your thoughts and prayers. We need action." And, while that is an understandable sentiment, it really misses the point of prayer: prayer brings divine and human action together toward creative solutions. Prayer is not us standing to the side just hoping for unilateral divine intervention. Prayer is a call for divine-human cooperation. Prayer brings the supernatural power of heaven into earth.

So, don't pray unless you want spectacular results. Don't ask God to endorse blinking timidity. "Father God, bless my business-as-usual." No way.

We have been trained to settle for less and then call it submission to the will of God. We resign ourselves to fate and call it humility. But, again, we walk by *faith*, not *fate*. God is actively searching for relentless people, people who refuse to sit by any longer and watch the world go to hell.

The heavenly Head Coach is actively recruiting players as we speak. Your current situation is like a high school game, and the coaching staff from Heaven U is watching you from the sidelines. How will you play the game? Are you relentless? Yes? Good. Then, the Big Guy's recruiting you to get in the game, the Big Game, the game that's being played on the world stage.

Everything you've been through so far has been prep for the big leagues. God is testing you to certify you. He wants to increase your capacity for spiritual warfare and kingdom dominion.

That job you hate? He placed you there to temper your spirit and strengthen your mettle.

The financial struggle you've faced? God uses money like modeling clay to teach you how to sculpt marble (Bill Johnson).

The family conflict? God is teaching you how to mediate and manifest peace on your home turf so you can carry it to the world.

The glory of God is weighty. Greater glory means greater responsibility. So, God is increasing your capacity for glory by testing you. He's stretching you. He wants to use you in a game that shifts the outcome of human history. Want to live a life that makes a difference? Then let him stretch you. Let him put you in the game.

How do we get in the game? We get in the game by getting involved, by taking action. But action without the power of the Holy Spirit is futile. Human action alone is demoralizing and disillusioning. So, when we make the decision to get in the game, we must start with three things:

(1) *Praise*: when we lift up exuberant worship, we enthrone God on our praise. (Psalm 22:3) The kingdom of God advances in the earth through praise. We shift atmospheres when we exalt the Lord over every situation.

(2) *Prayer*: when we pray, we bring heaven to earth. (Matthew 6:10) Prayer is a conduit through which the will of God is manifest. Prayer is more than petition; prayer is partnership. Effective prayer discovers the heart and mind of God and speaks it into the earth. As humans given dominion over the earth, we authorize divine action in the earth when we pray.

(3) *Prophecy*: when we declare the promises of God, we summon the future into present reality. Prophetic speech releases the promises of God into every situation. We must declare and decree what God has said. Prophecy is simply hearing what God is saying and speaking it into the world. We actually sow the atmosphere with words as seed. We reap whatever we sow.

Here's some Bonus Content on prophecy:

We go to war with the prophecies we have received. Paul told Timothy,

This charge I entrust to you, Timothy, my child, in accordance with the prophecies previously made about you, that by them you may wage the good warfare, holding faith and a good conscience. (1 Timothy 1:18–19)

It's a war of words.

Start by asking Jesus to speak to you. As Bill Johnson says, he is the Word of God, so he's always speaking. We just have to start listening. So, ask him to speak, then listen. He will talk to you from Scripture; from worship videos on YouTube; from nature—keep a sharp lookout for "signals" in nature; from your own heart; from conversation with others; and countless other ways.

When the Lord gives you a word, write it down. If someone shares a prophetic word with you, whip out your phone and record it. Keep a record of the prophecies declared over you so you can go to war with them.

Jeana keeps candy dishes scattered around our house overflowing with slips of paper that have prophetic words written on them. Anyone can grab one at any time and be encouraged. She also puts little chalkboards everywhere so anyone can scribble encouraging messages. That's what prophetic words *are* —encouraging words. (1 Corinthians 14:3)

We must steward prophecy. We must partner with the promises. When we hear a word declaring God's promise, we tend to lean back in our chair and wonder if it will happen. "Hmmm, I wonder if that's a true prophecy." But prophecies happen through *synergy*, through the power of *alignment* and *agreement*. So, when a word is given, the prophecy releases potential that is now available to us.

But we must believe the promise. We must partner with the word. When we believe the promise, we agree with the truth that God declares and we renounce the lie that opposes the truth. We have a *say* in the outcome. Literally.

You may have noticed already, but the *words* we speak are a huge part of getting in the game. The angel said to Daniel, "Your *words* have been heard, and I have come because of your *words*" (Daniel 10:12). Praise, prayer and prophecy are all Spirit-empowered words.

Speaking faith played a huge part in how we got saved in the first place.

> *"The word is near you, in your mouth and in your heart" (that is, the word of faith that we proclaim); because, if you confess with your mouth that Jesus is Lord and believe in your heart that God raised him from the dead, you will be saved. For with the heart one believes and is justified, and with the mouth one confesses and is saved. For the Scripture says, "Everyone who believes in him will not be put to shame." Believe in your heart and confess with your mouth. (Romans 10:8–11)*

Believing and confessing is how we got in the game. But it is also how we *stay* in the game. Believing and confessing are the basics of Christian faith. Believe the promises of God and confess them with your mouth. Everything in the kingdom of God works this way.

When you face a hopeless situation, do what Jesus said: Speak to the mountain. Read it carefully:

> *And Jesus answered them, "Have faith in God. Truly, I say to you, whoever says to this mountain, 'Be taken up and thrown into the sea,' and does not doubt in his heart, but believes that what he says will come to pass, it will be done for him. Therefore I tell you, whatever you ask in prayer, believe that you have received it, and it will be yours. (Mark 11:22–24)*

Zoom in on what Jesus said:

(1) *Speak to the mountain.* Like we used to tell our kids when they were little, "Use your words." Be specific. Say exactly what you want to see happen. And keep saying it until it happens.

(2) *Do not doubt in your heart.* How in the world do we do *that*?! This is not a trap. God is not tricking you. If you will turn your focus away from yourself and focus on declaring the promises of God, the doubt in your heart will evaporate in the

heat of God's word. Doubt is a thought; therefore, it only exists if you think it. Doubt only exists when you focus on it. Stop focusing on doubt and focus on God's promise, and doubt disappears.

(3) Believe that what you say—what you say!—will come to pass. Believe that there is divine power in the words of God spoken from your mouth. Believe that the same God who created the world with his word is now recreating your world with his word through what you say. *Speak the promises of God!*

How long do I keep speaking? Until the mountain moves.

But the mountain will not move until you move. You must respond to God's command to take the initiative through faith. You must open your mouth and speak the promises of God. Refuse to speak anything that God is not saying. We get the ball rolling when we speak faith.

Miracles start with movement. God always moves us to move. He moves us with a promise, and then moves us to respond. Again, people often think that divine intervention happens unilaterally, that God simply snaps his fingers and it is done. But this not true. God works through the world as it is. He works through the agency of angels at the invitation of people against the resistance of evil spirits. God works when we work. God moves when we move.

I once heard Bishop Jakes preach a message called, *Keep It Moving.* He quoted from the story of Israel crossing the Red Sea:

> *Then the Lord said to Moses, "Why are you crying out to me? Tell the Israelites to move on. Raise your staff and stretch out your hand over the sea to divide the water so that the Israelites can go through the sea on dry ground. (Exodus 14:15–16 NIV)*

"Tell the Israelites to move on." Powerful message.

As I've heard it put so many times, you can't steer a parked car. You just have to start. Every business leadership guru on the planet will tell you that "just getting started" is the hardest part. Most people will die with the better part of their dreams still in them, unfulfilled, all because they couldn't find the courage to swallow hard and just get started.

And once you get moving, you must keep moving. Miracles take time. I know there are occasions when God—SHAZAM!—answers your prayers all at once. But face it: that's rare, people. Usually, God drives in the slow lane. And that angry guy over there in the fast lane, riding bumpers and cussing slow drivers? That's you and me. While God takes his time.

God created the leisurely Sunday drive.

Partnership with God is not magic. We can't just fling an "abracadabra" at our problems. Partnership with God is a relationship. And relationships take time. God is more interested in *you* than he is the answer to your problem. Sometimes he will delay your answer because he wants to develop you. He wants to develop that "keep moving!" side of you, the side of you that becomes relentless and determined.

We think of faith as the ability to move God immediately. But Jesus described faith as the ability to keep asking even when answers don't come. Yes, he did! Look at the story:

> And he told them a parable to the effect that they ought always to pray and not lose heart. He said, "In a certain city there was a judge who neither feared God nor respected man. And there was a widow in that city who kept coming to him and saying, 'Give me justice against my adversary.' For a while he refused, but afterward he said to himself, 'Though I neither fear God nor respect man, yet because this widow keeps bothering me, I will give her justice, so that she will not beat me down by her continual coming.'"

> And the Lord said, "Hear what the unrighteous judge says. And will not God give justice to his elect, who cry to him day and night? Will he delay long over them? I tell you, he will give justice to them speedily. Nevertheless, when the Son of Man comes, will he find faith on earth?" (Luke 18:1–8)

We "ought always to pray and not lose heart." The faith Jesus is looking for when he returns is persevering faith, faith that refuses to slouch off the field in defeat. Faith that stays in the game until the tide turns and the enemy is pushed back through end zone.

God moves when we move. Think about your favorite Sunday School stories. In every one, without exception, God moved when his people moved:

- Moses lifts his rod; God divides the sea.

- The servants fill the pots with water; Jesus turns the water to wine.

- David swings his slingshot; God guides the stone.

- Peter steps out of the boat; Jesus helps him walk on water.

- The people roll away the stone; Jesus raises Lazarus.

- The widow fills the pots with oil; God multiplies it.

- The widow feeds Elijah first (!); her food never runs out again.

- Jesus tells the man, "Take up your bed and walk"; he does, and he is totally healed.

- Bartimaeus cast off his beggar's garments; Jesus healed his blindness.

Can you think of more? There are hundreds more.

In every story, people were called to step out on faith before the miracle happened. This is how God works. We have to get in the game before we can win the game. You're already losing if you're sitting in the stands. *Get in the game!*

How often have I awakened in the morning in the grip of suffocating anxiety, imagining a future so bleak and dreadful that I feel panic rising like a toxic fog. Hopeless scenarios claw over each other, swarming my mind with fear and doubt. As Kris Vallotton says, "Hopelessness is imagining a future without God," and in that moment of morning dread, all I can see in my future is me failing, me not having enough, being enough, knowing enough, doing well enough. Me, me, me. Never enough.

Then I hear the gentle voice of the Holy Spirit, "Where is Jesus in your imagined future?" And I stop to think about it. Where is he? There he is, right there in the middle of every situation, working, loving, caring, healing, delivering, providing, guiding, doing whatever is needed to give me victory in all things. And in the instant that I see him in my future, hope rises. The instant that I stop looking at *me* and start looking at him.

Stop worrying about the future. Start dreaming about the future. Imagine what God will do in your future. You are not a helpless bystander watching as fate determines your future. You have a role to play in the outcome. Use your words. Speak faith into every scenario. Envision Jesus in every scenario. Daydream about what God will do in you, through you and for you.

Seattle Seahawks quarterback, Russell Wilson, one of the greatest athletes playing the game right now, tells of how he approaches every game by closing his eyes and visualizing every play. He thinks back on the opposing team videos he's studied the week before, and he imagines every play from the opening kick to the final seconds of the game. He walks through the scenarios in his mind, finding weaknesses in his team's play and adjusting his game to correct the errors. Wilson says it is truly amazing how much his visualization plays out to be true in the actual game.

You should do the same. Shut down fearful imaginations—we innocuously call it "worry"—and focus on imaginations sketched in faith and colored with hope. Dream big!

Imagine scenarios where every obstacle is overcome by the mighty power of God. Visualize armies of holy angels streaking across the sky like lightning. Look at the towering clouds gathering in the morning sky and imagine they are angel armies moving unstoppably through enemy resistance. Visualize the war and watch God win.

Where are you in the battle? Standing with your hands lifted high, giving God praise, interceding with powerful prayers and prophesying to the wind: "Blow, O wind of God, and drive back the enemies!" There you are, releasing healing, deliverance, provision through *your* words.

Where are you? You are *in the game*, refusing to stand by and watch outcomes go to hell. You are partnering with the mighty power of God, releasing the rule of Jesus into the earth through your increasing, insistent faith, faith that simply will not let go.

Imagine it all. Visualize it. If you think about, you're already visualizing—you're just visualizing the wrong things. That's what worry *is*—visualizing hopeless outcomes. So change what you see. Change what you dream about. Visualize victory. Visualize prosperity. Visualize healing. Visualize reconciliation. Look at your problem, whatever it is, and then imagine the God-promised outcome.

As I'm writing these final words, *See A Victory* by Elevation Worship is playing in my headphones. Wow. I cannot imagine a better soundtrack for these words.

"I'm gonna see a victory, I'm gonna see a victory;

for the battle belongs to you, Lord."

Did you get that? I'm gonna *see* a victory. But here's what I'm hearing: before I can *see* a victory, I have to *see* a victory. I have to *see* it in my heart before I can *see* it in my life. Long before I see the victory manifest, I have to see it in my Spirit-filled imagination.

I'm gonna see a victory. Long before I see a victory in my life, I'm gonna see it in my mind. I'm going to imagine it as I pray, as I dream with God, as I push back every lie that threatens my peace.

Long before the money manifests, I'm going to see prosperity in my heart.

Long before the wayward child returns home, I'm going to see dinner around the table with all my kids.

Long before culture shifts, I'm gonna see a transformed city and nation in my heart.

Long before human trafficking and slavery is finally and fully eradicated in the earth, I'm gonna see all people forever free in my heart.

I'm gonna imagine, like the Beatles sang, but I will not imagine a dreadful, empty world with no God, as they sang; rather, I will imagine a world empowered with the supernatural Presence of God, a world transformed by his love.

Whether I'm dreaming of global, big-picture problems, or soul-crushing crises much closer to home, I refuse to dream of a scenario that has no God in it. I refuse to dream of a scenario that has no miracles in it. I refuse to dream of a scenario that simply accepts the status quo. I refuse to dream of a scenario where I am just an observer. I intend to *get in the game!*

No more *"whatever."* No more *Que Sera, Sera.* No way. I have a role to play. I have a game to win. The world is waiting for someone to offer hope. As Bill Johnson says, "The person in the room with most hope has the most influence." The world is waiting for someone to offer solutions, and the solutions lie within our partnership with God.

Will you join me? The game requires a team. Will join the team? Will you join me as we praise, pray and prophesy? Will you make a commitment with me that we will never again sit in the stands and grumble about the score? Will you?

Yes, you will, in Jesus' name.

It's time to *get in the game.*

"It is not the critic who counts; not the man who points out how the strong man stumbled or where the doer of deeds could have done them better. The credit belongs to the man who is actually in the arena, whose face is marred by dust and sweat and blood; who strives valiantly; who errs and comes short again and again; who knows great enthusiasms, the great devotions; who spends himself in a worthy cause; who at the best, knows in the end the triumph of high achievement, and who, at the worst, if he fails, at least fails while daring greatly so that his place shall never be with those timid souls who neither know victory nor defeat."

— *Theodore Roosevelt*

ABOUT THE AUTHOR

 Steve Pixler lives with his wife, Jeana, and their six children in Mansfield, TX. Steve serves as Lead Pastor at Freedom Life Church, also in Mansfield.

To learn more about Steve's story, his writings and other ministry resources, visit stevepixler.com.

Made in the USA
Monee, IL
08 May 2021